Finlay is a visionary as well ... ...aster practitioner and a psychic me... ... is built around his insights into the world that ...ounds us and his research into the various components that make up our world. This book is the result of not only this research, but Finlay's ability to 'tap' into nature and the understandings brought by thousands of years of natural instincts.

For my mother and father.

Finlay McArthur

THE HUMAN WHISPERER

AUSTIN MACAULEY PUBLISHERS™
LONDON · CAMBRIDGE · NEW YORK · SHARJAH

Copyright © Finlay McArthur (2020)

The right of Finlay McArthur to be identified as author of this work has been asserted by him in accordance with section 77 and 78 of the Copyright, Designs and Patents Act 1988.

All rights reserved. No part of this publication may be reproduced, stored in a retrieval system, or transmitted in any form or by any means, electronic, mechanical, photocopying, recording, or otherwise, without the prior permission of the publishers.

Any person who commits any unauthorised act in relation to this publication may be liable to criminal prosecution and civil claims for damages.

This book is for general information purposes and nothing contained in it is, or is intended to be construed as advice. It does not take into account your individual health, medical, physical or emotional situation or needs. It is not a substitute for medical attention, treatment, examination, advice, treatment of existing conditions or diagnosis and is not intended to provide a clinical diagnosis nor take the place of proper medical advice from a fully qualified medical practitioner.

A CIP catalogue record for this title is available from the British Library.

ISBN 9781528983808 (Paperback)
ISBN 9781528983815 (ePub e-book)

www.austinmacauley.com

First Published (2020)
Austin Macauley Publishers Ltd
25 Canada Square
Canary Wharf
London
E14 5LQ

To all those who have encouraged me to sit down and write my thoughts for a second book, thank you!

Table of Contents

Synopsis 11

Chapter One 13
What is a Whisperer?

Chapter Two 21
Understanding Nature

Chapter Three 34
Invisible Energy

Chapter Four 45
Life of Meaning

Chapter Five 56
Your Life in This world

Chapter Six 66
Birth of Consciousness

Chapter Seven 81
Human Being

Chapter Eight 99
Who Am I?

Chapter Nine 109
What Am I Capable of?

Chapter Ten 124
Learn

Chapter Eleven 138
Ancient Ways of the Shaman

Chapter Twelve 151
Imagination

Chapter Thirteen 171
Senses

Conclusion 179

The Last Spark 181

Synopsis

The Human Whisperer is based around getting the reader engaged in looking at their world from another aspect. There have been books written about horse whisperers and dog whisperers which are designed to help people understand the behaviours and characteristics of dogs, horses and other animals that cannot communicate with us through speech. These books are great in the fact they give pointers to help us understand why a horse, dog or animals, in general, do what they do and what we can do to correct some of these behaviours.

Why then am I using a term like a whisperer to help you to understand us as humans? I feel we struggle at times to understand us, why we do what we do, and why we behave in the way we do. This book is going to try and take away the layers of our confusion and help the reader understand who we are and where we are heading as humans.

We will look at what a whisperer is, dive into the psyche and see that thoughts carry energy and that this energy can have an effect on not only things around us, but also on those around us. It will cover nature and how nature is an important part of us and that we cannot just go through life ignoring that aspect that allows us to survive as a race of people. It covers what meaning of life may be as it will encourage the reader to look at this important part of who they are. To do that, we need to understand the conscious part of us, so we look at the birth of consciousness and the confusion that science and history still have around this important part of who we are. I would like to think it brings in a new awareness of what a human being really is. This will allow the reader to grow and look, and encourage and engage with new experiences as they travel through their lives. I have tried to write the book in a simple basic way that will allow readers of all ages to understand the pages and contents.

Chapter One
What is a Whisperer?

There have been books written about horse whisperers and dog whisperers which are designed to help people understand the behaviours and characteristics of dogs, horses and other animals that cannot communicate with us through speech. Although I feel animals can communicate with us better than some humans I know. These books are great in the fact they give pointers to help us understand why a horse, dog or animals in general do what they do and what we can do to correct some of these behaviours.

Why then am I using a term like whisperer to help us understand us as humans? Well, simply I feel we struggle at times to understand us, why we do what we do and why we behave in the way we do. This book is going to try and take away the layers of our existence and help you to see who we are and where we are heading. Some of it will be an eye opener, some of it you already know and there will also be parts of it that will make you stop and realise that you have more effect on your life and those of others than you thought. Because everything you say or even think has an effect on everyone else around you. How? Because everything transmits through that quantum energy soup that connects us all to everything around you. Other humans, animals and even plant life. Hard to believe, eh? That what you think or feel not only affects us humans but things such as plant life, but believe me, it does. Research has proven that if you speak kindly to plants and show them love and gratitude, they respond by growing stronger and harder. Speak harshly to them, treat them with contempt and hatred and they will simply wither and eventually die. If we can have that effect on plants, then we can affect everything else around us in exactly the same way. There have been interesting experiments done by the likes of Dr Masaru Emote where water was put into two glass vessels each the same height and made the same way with the same about of water in each vessel. Then labels were put on the vessels and placed where people could read them. On one vessel he wrote, negative words. On the other he wrote, love, compassion and other kind and heart felt words. He left them there for a couple of days, then took them back to his lab. The water molecules in the vessel with negative words written on it had begun to densify. They didn't move around in the vessel easily the shapes had changed and took on peaks and troughs, they were heavy and moved in an awkward way. The water in the other vessel, the one with love and compassion and other nice words written on it, saw the molecules moved easily, they moved with purpose and their shape was smooth and almost perfect.

Now for me what makes that experiment incredible is that people didn't touch the jars they simply read the words written on them and then projected onto the water thoughts and feelings associated with those words. That was a real time experiment you can read for yourself on the internet. What is amazing is that the water took on the emotions projected onto them. So, if you stop and think, are we passing onto others, as well as ourselves the emotions we think and say. After all people in the above experiment, well most anyway, didn't say anything out loud they simply read and projected their thoughts quietly on to the water. Isn't that simply mind blowing? Your thoughts alone can change water molecules, so imagine if you are interacting with someone, what you are thinking may have an effect on that person or person's psyche and theirs may be affecting yours without you realising. In fact, the very thoughts you are thinking either positive or negative does affect people, animals and plants and indeed as we have seen, water. Next time you are having a chat with someone and you are thinking negative thoughts about them remember that it could have a negative impact on the psyche of the person you are speaking with. Especially when you think we are 60–70% water, what impact could negative thoughts and feelings have on the molecular structure of us, since we are mostly water and carbon based? Interesting thought, eh?

There have been experiments carried out in the USA where volunteers donate tissue samples which are then kept alive under lab conditions. The donor is taken away to another room or another part of the facility. The donor is then subjected to stress or indeed pleasure. The tissue sample has been known to react to that stimuli, even though it's no longer a part of that person and is several feet away from its host. So again, it proves that we are connected to us and the world around us even though we think we are separate, we are all connected in many ways yet to be discovered. The point of this is that what we think and how we act affects everything around us in ways we are still discovering. Next time you feel negative just stop and think how much of what is around you is also being affected negatively due to these feelings you are putting out there into the world. Likewise, your negativity could be something that you are picking up unconsciously from your surroundings.

That was a mind opening start to this book, wasn't it? Life is here to be explored but not just the physical, but also that part of us that we are just beginning to understand. And 'that's the main aim of this book, just like the animals and pets around us who struggle to communicate, actually sorry, who WE struggle to understand, the aim is to get you to look at different parts of who we are so we can try to understand the bigger picture. Just like people who have a knack of knowing what our dogs, cats and horses etc., are trying to communicate with us. In my other book, *Get Out of Your Way* we looked at what is stopping you from moving forward to the life you want, we looked at beliefs, fears, comfort zones and recognise that it may just be us/you that is the block you from getting what you want. In this book I would like you to open your mind even more by now understanding that when you have understood yourself a little better, you can then comprehend the world around you. This book is simply that, as we understood from our friend William of Ockham the simplest assumption should be taken when looking at two competing theories, as we, humans do like to complicate matters. As such we will, as we did in the other book, take the straightest forward approach.

We are the masks we wear, the guise we put on when going out into the world, that can confuse those around us. In my lifetime I can safely say I have met just two people that gave me a sense of they knew who they were. No masks, no hiding behind the trappings of society they were just them. I find it a humbling experience to understand someone from being, well, simply them.

Now, first little exercise you can do when you are quiet and peaceful, and this may resonate in the deepest part of us, ask yourself which people you have met in your life so far that you can truly say you know them unconditionally? That you know them for who they are, not for who they are either pretending to be or think they should be in the world. It's a bit deep I know but ask yourself that question and make a note of it. Why do I ask that? Well, if you do the exercise honestly you will already know. Basically, I bet there are not many people you really know for who they truly are. And yes, I also mean family members, teachers, best friends and close associates. We think we are complex creatures and we then go out and portray that to the world. We are the world around us, but we are not what we think the world around us is. Big difference and this is where the 'whisperer' comes in, we need to understand what the world of nature is showing us, we need to understand the language she speaks to us in. Yes, I am still calling nature a she, just fits right for me. All sounds a bit hippy, but perhaps the hippy culture had some of it right. To be a whisperer means that you need to recognise the behaviours of the subject you are working with, sorry don't mean to call animals or humans subjects, but you know what I mean. In this case your life, those in it and nature around you are the subject. All you need to do is understand the signs to lead you to a better and perhaps deeper awareness of you. Shamans have known this for thousands of years and some practicing today still know how to read the signs and follow where they lead. We all have this instinct, it's just history and life has evolved at such an incredibly fast rate that we, as a collective race, have forgotten some of these old and I feel important ways of being. I am not talking about any theoretical teachings, but I am talking about how our ancient ancestors lived and communicated with nature, the ways majority of us have forgotten. I am hoping that this book will bring some of these old approaches to the consciousness and perhaps make you stop and become a part of being a 'human whisperer' that we all were years ago, or maybe it should be called 'nature whisperer'.

A wonderful North American native friend of mine reminded me that in their ancient laws and traditions, we are a part of nature, and nature and the world is a part of us. They knew and lived by these ideas and thoughts long before we arrived as a supposed 'civilised culture'. Interestingly, one of the oldest religious people on the planet the Pagans also believed and lived by the same thoughts and ideas as their North American cousins did not realising that each other existed.

In light of that, it is thoughtful to me that if they didn't know each other existed and yet lived by the same rules and ideas, who told them about it? North America, South Americans, ancient Europeans and ancient tribes of the Indian subcontinent lived and thrived by the same ideas as each other, thousands of years before Christianity arrived. As mentioned, I find it incredible that they all listened to nature and the seasons, they knew of a greater power at work which we like to call the universe. They seemed to understand it and work with it and knew the secrets which we have long forgotten. Let's try and unlock some of these old ideas and theories and use them to make our modern lives a little more meaningful. Hence the whisperer idea, that we can become attuned to the world around us in ways that we didn't know existed, or perhaps have forgotten over time, as we move forward in our technological lives. I love the theories that quantum physics are now coming up with, that our ancients already seemed to know and understand thousands of years ago. So, why are we now relying on science to bring back and prove, that these old ways of living actually made sense. Maybe because people may feel that gap widening between nature and our modern technological world.

More and more people are now, as mentioned in my first book, looking for answers to certain aspects of their lives to which they don't know where to look. Perhaps as life becomes easier and technology takes an ever-increasing hold on our lives, we are forgetting the natural part of our lives of who we are. I think there is a nagging part of all of us that is getting increasingly confused as more of who we are is being taken away by technology and we find ourselves not being able to think for ourselves, as mobile phone, tablets, computers etc. do our thinking for us. Common sense seems to be faltering, a sense of being is also shifting and it is that control that I think people are trying to hang onto. I doubt many of us realise just how much we are giving up to the way things are becoming. Some people I speak to state that they don't feel in control anymore and feel like they are relinquishing responsibility of their lives to others. And as we know, if you 'don't take responsibility for your own actions, your life and your part in it, then you are giving it up to others that like to control and tell you what to do. That's why in writing this book I hope you open your mind and heart and listen to your psyche, to what may be missing in your world. I am mentioning psyche because I feel that's where we store out thoughts and emotions. A dictionary meaning is:

Another word for the place where your thoughts come from is your psyche. Not your actual brain, but whatever it is that generates all of your thoughts and emotions. Psyche comes from the Greek psyche, which means 'the soul, mind, spirit, or invisible animating entity which occupies the physical body'.

Some may also say it's your subconscious and yes, I also agree, but for now we are going to use psyche. As I get it that the Greeks were switched onto this part of our being thousands of years ago, which follows on from the above when I mentioned that the ancients knew about this long before we use modern science to understand it.

This book then will hopefully by its design, make you stop and think, it may open up your mind to other thoughts and questions. I want it to tap into nature as within nature we find a lot of the answers you may be looking for. And yes, this all sounds a little deep and a little hippy, but then why not, the hippy movement back in the 60s and 70s didn't do any harm and the free love it brought didn't start wars. Yes, I know it brought other things into play which I don't agree with.

But at least people then were exploring themselves beyond the boundaries of modern society.

What I want to achieve at the end of this opus is to give you an understanding that you have the ability to retune into the person we were years ago. You know when a cat or dog or other kind of animal is hungry, wants to go out or indeed just wants a cuddle or play. You know what they want by looking at them, as you understand their behaviour, you didn't study cat or dog at school, but you instinctively know what they need or are asking for. Well that's what I hope to achieve at the end of this book, to give you that ability to look around you and, using your instincts, know what is happening within nature, with others and more importantly, within yourself.

The important message here is to look, you see we look with our eyes, we take on board what we are physically looking at, but we have, or some of us, lost the ability to look beyond the seeing to what is really happening. Obviously, it's important to see physically as otherwise we would bump into things, but we also need to look beyond that into the realm of the unseen, the unphysical the psyche to understand what's really going on. I apologise here to the blind as I know they cannot see the physical, but some I have met are already tapping this unseen, by using their instincts to get a view of the world they cannot physically see. I admire them so much for this and we can learn from them in how to use this sixth sense to navigate through the physical world.

In this chapter, we have just had a look at what you can expect from the coming pages. Is this a spiritual book? Maybe, it's not intending to be, but it's just a simple book in getting you to open your eyes, mind and giving you the insight in having a proper look at the world around you. As we navigate through the next new few chapters, I hope it may resonate with you in that deep part of the mind, that we have shut off, as this modern society with all its trappings, has made us forget that we are part of a bigger picture. As the first chapter, I hope that this has whetted your appetite and as we begin to read through the forthcoming chapters, as always, keep that mind open, keep fluid and just allow your thoughts to look beyond the normal.

Chapter Two
Understanding Nature

The first part of looking at nature is getting back to basics. We all know that when we look around us nature is the birds, animals, trees, plants, sky, water etc. As we can see that and understand it, well in most part we do, so then let's look at us, as nature. What do I mean us as nature? Well, the first part of understanding where we fit in the great scheme of things, is we need to identify the essence of what makes us apart of nature, and that simply is us, who we are, our mind, body and spirit. You see without a mind or spirit a body is just a body. Without a spirit the body and mind become one without reason, and a body and spirit without a mind has no direction. We need all three to become who we are. I believe, and this is just an assumption, that our spirit is becoming lessen as we listen to those around us. Our minds are becoming confused with the ramblings of modern-day societies, news, media and people telling us what is and isn't good for us. Our bodies are becoming trapped as we become too perfect in what we eat and drink as our natural bodily defences are being depleted and we have to rely on supplements to replenish the good natural bacteria that we should find within us. The spirit part of us is trying to point out that we are, at times of course, not who we think we are as what we think we are is being pushed back into our psyche as we listen and believe what others tell us who we should be. Why are we trying to be who we believe we should be? Well, that's due to the fact we feel we have to conform to the world around us and have lost the ability to be an individual. We fail to listen to our basic instincts as we do not allow our spirit-selves to bring us back into alignment.

Let's look at this another way as I believe it is important. The body is needed to move the minds ideas thoughts and theories around the physical plane. The mind is needed to make sense of the world around us, to break down the ideas presented to us through life's many mediums and then to give us a sense of self and our sense of our place within this life. The spirit is that, behind the scenes, part of our psyche that lets us experience and become a part of the physical world we are in now at any given moment on this planet. But at the same time absorbs both the mind and body experiences and holds it within a non-physical library that we can use at any time to make sense of our true world experience. Unfortunately, we don't use this library very often and when that old tiger appears (as referenced in the first book) we run around looking for answers and asking why me? The idea is to use the spirit or subconscious and tap into it every day and realise this immense power and information which is at hand anytime we need it.

As we are all spiritual beings having a human experience, we allow the physical body and mind to make sense of the experiences we have every second, minute, hour etc. And as we know we store on a conscious basis about seven million bits of information ever second. Our mind sets the fences and boundaries of what we think we are capable of doing or achieving. The body then carries us around the world fuelled and driven by what the mind thinks we are each individually competent of. That in turn is inspired by our non-physical spirit. However, as most of us are inspired by the mind with its boundaries and fences, instead of letting the spirit in, to guide us through our lives and really show what we can do. We allow the mind to guide us and that is why we may struggle, as the mind is limited and builds blockages, where the spirit doesn't know of any boundaries and breaks down blockages to open up our minds to possibilities, to which the body responds by taking us on these amazing physical journeys, if we let it.

The above is an opening to what we mean by letting in nature and being a part of the bigger picture. To be a part of nature is to realise that we are nature, as mentioned above it's not out there in what we see, it is within and apart of who we are. So why do we distance ourselves from the one thing that we are a part of? I believe that we have forgotten who we are where we came from and as a result, so many people are feeling they don't belong, they feel disconnected as they have pushed away the natural or nature state and allowed themselves to be a part of a society with shallow views and opinions being led to believe they are disconnected. If we allow ourselves the privilege of realising that we are all connected to a higher spiritual source, one of infinite possibilities and one of understanding you can do anything you put your mind to? Doesn't that make sense? To those other feelings of being alone, unloved and one of giving the impression that we are locked into a person that struggles to achieve or even to realise its goals, wants and happiness?

Before we go on what do I actually mean by spirit, as I realise that it may mean different things to different people. What I mean by the spiritual self is that unseen force that drives us from a subconscious point of view. It's that powerful part of us that takes on in excess of 17+ million bits of information every second. It's that part of us that tries to be heard over the noise and clutter of everyday life. It is that part of us that is bigger and more powerful than we can imagine at this time of our personal evolution and growth. You cannot see it, you cannot physically hear it nor smell it. Its untouchable and has no taste, but you can sense it when you are quiet and you let it speak to you. It's those gut feelings, that part of you that guides you quietly to a different level of existence if you allow it. It gives you challenges and also helps you with the solutions and gives you that inner strength to achieve the impossible. But it's that latter that we don't listen to, as we rely too much on our physical senses, on what we hear, taste, touch, smell and see, which we have covered previously.

How does nature help us and why should we take the time to be connected with it? Those who think that nature is nothing more than the world out there beyond the front room window, or things they see on the television should take note that nature is having an effect on them every second of every moment. Just take a look at the earth/moon cycles and what they mean to us.

I was on holiday in Tuscany a few years back and we went on a vineyard tour. I mean it's rude not to know more about the wine I was consuming most nights, right? So, we went on this tour it was late summer and the owner was telling us about the grape varieties he had on the vineyard.

There was a couple with us from England a farming couple who took some time away from their busy schedules for a nice weekend in Italy. The gentleman of this couple, asked the owner when he pruned the vines, now I was excepting him to say in the autumn or late winter. However, the answer he gave puzzled me, he said I cut the vines back when we have a waning moon.

I asked why in a waning moon phase? He answered as that's when the plant fluids are pulled back into the earth thus making it safer for the plants if I cut them back during a waning moon. That fascinated me and more so when the farmer answered, "Ah! Yes, I cut the horns of the bulls also during a waning moon." I asked why and he stated that during a waning moon the bulls do not bleed as much as they would if I cut their horns during a waxing moon, how amazing is that?

I did some more research and it appears trees are cut during a waning moon when the sap is at its lowest, or drawn down into the earth, so I did further research about how this phenomenon affects us as humans. It appears a lot of study has been done about the moon and how it affects us during its typical 29.5-day cycle. What crosses my mind is if plant fluids and the blood in animals is drawn down during a waning moon and we are mostly water, could it be that our life fluids are also drawn down during a waning moon? It is also interesting to read that 'lunacy' is from the Latin word for *Luna* describing the moon. The ancients, including Aristotle, believed that health and mental issues were caused by a waning mood as the gravitational affect had an influence on the body's fluids. Now I will add that majority of scientific research concludes that the moon has no influence over our moods at all. However, the ancients had other ideas and indeed wrote about the effect the moon had on nature, when seeds should be planted, when a harvest should take place, when cattle and other farmed animals should be induced etc. It seems then, that there may be some conflicting issues between the ancients and modern science. I decided to ask some more questions around the pruning of plants. Another vineyard I visited and asked the questions when they prune, the answer was during a waning moon, I said but surely that's superstition. He said no, once they cut the vines during a waxing moon and the crop that year was not as good as the previous years when they followed the tradition of cutting during a waning moon. I asked that perhaps the conditions that year wasn't as good, he said, "Yes, they were, in fact better than the preceding years." From that moment, we always prune during a waning phase. I will leave you with this thought, that why do the ancients and those working on the land day in, day out all year long, work with the moon phases as they know and believe that this will have an effect on their produce and lively hoods, in fact their lives. Yet we, that live away from that environment, do not take any notice of what kind of moon it is. Perhaps we should take more notice and work around these phases, which may help us with what we decide, what we do what action we take and how we think! Interesting thought that nature does have an effect on us 24/7, 365 days of the year and perhaps more than we think. I did some further study and it seems that turtles, toads and other waterborne animals follow these phases to breed and lay their eggs. This is just one aspect of nature that, without us really knowing, guides our minds and psyche but if you can tap into all that nature provides can you imagine what is on offer. Take time out now and again and just be quiet in nature, in the woods, by a lake, on a hilltop in a meadow even, it doesn't matter, but just take time to be quiet and listen and try to connect.

I will hasten to add that the people mentioned above are not pink and fluffy, nor from a hippy background (sorry hippies) or from some research base. They are just normal people that have found a way or grown up in a way of being with nature. Working with her, being her servant and listening to what she has to say. The ancients did it and a lot of people still do. They are not from a mystic tribe or from some cult following, they are people who have learned to work and listen to her. I remember my grandmother in Scotland could tell what the weather was going to do by looking at the hills at the back of their house. I would say Auntie, it's going to rain later according to the weather forecast. She would look at the hills, although I never did find out what she was actually looking at, but she would say nope, it's going to stay fine. And she was right ten out of ten, she always knew just by a simple glance at the distant hills. As my 'gift' grew, I also found myself doing the same thing when I was younger. I could always tell when the weather was going to change when the seasons would come and what the year had in store. I still do and it still amazes me how accurate it can be. Those who know me will testify that that I am not pink and fluffy, nor spend hours studying the weather patterns. However, I do spend time just being outside in nature and taking time to observe her as she ebbs and flows through the days, weeks and months. In fact, a premonition, as I write this now, which is beginning of April 2018, I believe that this summer will be very dry to start with, getting very warm, with a wetter end to it.

So the seasons, now interestingly enough science has proved that we do suffer during the seasons and especially in early autumn when the daylight is getting less, the weather is getting colder and things like vitamin D which we get during the summer months from the sun lessens. People suffer from things like SAD (Seasonal Affective Disorder) where they don't get enough daylight. Our bodies go through a physical change. Not enough for most to realise, but people actually produce less serotonin, which is a hormone that regulates things like mood, our feelings of happiness and wellbeing which gets disrupted during the winter months when there 'isn't as much sunlight as there is during the summer and spring months. So then, in the winter we can become a little down and not feeling at our best. In that case the late autumn and winter can affect us, interestingly it also affects the plants and other organic matter during this darker colder cycle. I read in a report years ago that we haven't developed enough as a race of people not to hibernate during the winter months, and that leading up to the wintertime, we store more fat ready to sleep for the duration.

Well, anyway that's my excuse. But seriously, if that's true, then the seasons and again nature is having that effect on us, on our bodies and our minds. Perhaps we have lost the ability to understand why we, at times of the year, act and behave slightly differently to other times of the year. Get those children playing in the outdoors, put those horrible PlayStations away and let their minds interact with nature. I may be as bold to say that, I was born in wonderful age that was allowing individual children's minds to develop with imaginations, the weather, playing in the forests, meadows and climbing trees. I came home filthy dirty, but with a sense of wonder when using my imagination, I built a camp to protect us from the cowboys and Indians which made me feel excited and worthy. It's not always the case, but these days I notice children playing with mobile phones, mobile tablets and PlayStations that provide the entertainment so that they don't have to think or use their amazing imaginations. It does worry me a little that in ten or twenty-years' time what will their minds be tuned into – an open, elastic, flowing imagination kind of mind or one that cannot think for itself unless stimulated by some kind of electronic stimulus?

How did the ancients manage to live without all this technology? Very well, I would say. Things like Stonehenge, the pyramids, Chichen Itza. Even more modern cities like Venice, Rome ancient London, Jerusalem, Petra. All these places built without computers or technology and most still standing today. What did they use to build these amazing places? Their imaginations and then common sense which allowed their minds to be flexible and fluid to work out ways around problems caused by some of the issues of 'ancient' construction. That's what I mean, the ability to work things out for yourself.

Sorry I digress, but going back to nature, the ancients knew when the weather was going to break, when the seasons would change and using the sun, moon and what nature could and would provide, they not only survived but they grew and became successful. North American indigenous tribes had a unique way of appreciating the four elements of air, fire, earth and water which make up the basics of nature. They believed that these four elements were alive within their worlds and each element was an individual spirit and each had to be in balance in order for not only nature, but for these tribes to survive and prosper. They would take time too bless and honour these individual elements and to recognise the characters within them. But as Denise Linn points out in her book, *Kindling the Native Spirit*, in our modern-day culture we don't engage with these elements because we only identify with the limited boundaries of our bodies. And I couldn't agree more, as unless we engage with all aspects, we limit ourselves to us, our individual being.

Now, I also agree that we need to understand our individual being as otherwise we won't allow our sense of consciousness to grow and learn, which in my first book, *Get Out of Your Way* explains. But, it's the combined understanding of both that will allow us to really grow and comprehend the vastness of the universe and the part we play within it.

As mentioned, all we have to do is take time to be in nature, open your minds to her, let her guide you and show you what you could achieve. In doing so, I believe that we may become healthier in mind and body and certainly richer in our lives as we begin to understand that all we need is out there. There is a price for destroying nature, the diminishing rain forests in South America is causing us to have weather problems. Pollution is causing crops to fail and certain parts of nature like insects that we need to survive, to die causing an imbalance. This isn't going to become a sermon on destroying our planet, but it is meant to make you realise that nature does have an effect on you, your health and your being more than you realise. All you have to do is start to take note that part of nature that is around you, learn from her and help her to help you. Open your mind and understand that she provides almost everything you need to survive on this planet of ours, understanding something that helps you to survive is, I would consider important.

To recap, we have seen how something like the moon phases could have an effect on your being as its waxes and wanes. The seasons also play an important part in how we feel as the different hormones within us change to the beat of winter, spring, summer and autumn. Getting outside and having fun in the open air may give you that sense of wellbeing and the shot of those all-important vitamins the sun gives us. Perhaps take time to look back at how the ancient civilisations used nature and understood her being. I talk about nature as a her, as for me that makes sense that she provides for us as a mother would. I also think she has a soul; no, I haven't been drinking. Because animals, plants, trees the weather and us, react to her as we have seen above. This is just an appetite teaser for you to discover more about how 'mother nature' affects you. Take time to understand and to feel her as she moves around you and enters your life on a daily basis. I have friends that live and work in London, when I talk about this, they say that's all very well if you live in the country but we live in the city. Understand it doesn't matter where you live country, village, town or city nature affects you at all levels 24/7, 365 days of the year. If you live in a city or town, just take time to look at the nature around you, the 'trees, the birds, open green areas, the parks. Just get outdoors look and see what's around you, it is all there to be discovered and more importantly, to be felt and engaged with. It is not pink and fluffy, it's a fact, try it, I know you want to, and you will be amazed at what you discover about you and the world around you.

Another part too connecting to nature is the messages that come from her or our higher selves that we dismiss. I am talking about messages brought to us by the use of animals, or the use of animal totems. This may bring you important messages or just some guidance on where you are right now. Yes, I hear you say, more hippy crap. (Sorry, hippies, I don't mean to use you as a medium to get the point across it's just people can relate to that 'fluffy' nature, examples I use) but you couldn't be further from the truth. I use them and see them on a daily basis.

I have a Red Kite totem that is with me a lot and especially when I sit down to write. You see I always start to stutter a little when I being to write, then almost 90% of the time I hear the kite and what does the kite represent – *take of your mask and let the world know who you really are.*

I really relate to that as when I started my first book, I admit to being a little shy in letting the world know more about me. Hearing the kite really, honestly helped me in opening up.

As I was making my mind up about whether to write my first book or not, I was walking down the driveway to my house and nearly jumped out of my skin, as there on the wall next to my driveway was a tawny owl, that hooted at me and just watched me for a while. I watched it for ages which was probably only a few seconds, I then carried on to my front door, went to open it and as I turned around it flew quietly and gently off into the dusky night. What does the owl represent – *This is a particularly ripe time to tap into the fount of intuitive wisdom that's available to you.* A couple of days later I started putting together my first book, and you know what, I had more inside of me to start the book than I realised. Last year was a very poignant time of my life for many reasons. At this particular point I was getting too involved with a specific part of my life that just wasn't working, but at the time I wasn't aware just how draining it was becoming. I was walking in a lovely park near where I live at a point where my shoelace worked its way lose. I saw a tree trunk just the right height for me to put my shoe on to tie it up. Next to the tree trunk I saw a bush, not sure what kind it was, but it was blooming and smelt lovely. Then my gaze turned to a truly astonishing sight, there on a twig near one of the blooming flowers, was a praying mantis. Just sitting quietly, I couldn't believe my eyes, I had no idea we have them in this country. I knew they are common in some European countries but had no idea they were in this country. I later found out that there are some but not common in this area. Now I went on this walk to try and clear my head from the present clutter I was experiencing, and at that point I had to tie my shoe; there was this amazing insect sitting quietly but majestically on a twig in the bush. I watched it for a while, then realised that it may actually be bringing me a message. I rushed home and looked it up in my animal totem book and the message was simply: *consider redirecting your energy from something that isn't working and give greater focus and attention to that which is working. Listen to your instincts as to when to move forward and when to retreat.* That was it, a simple message but to me a powerful one in that it shocked me from that present state and allowed me to look at changing things and, as the message said, to redirect my energy. I did just that and things began to change quite quickly. One last example, I was going on a trip, one I wasn't looking forward to and I was, perhaps, moaning a little about it. Well, okay, moaning a big bit about it. I was in the garden siting down reading and a wasp came buzzing toward me, as usual I waved my arms about in a vain attempt to warn it off, but it was a little persistent, so I just sat still. The cheeky little thing sat on my nose, needless to say I thought here we go one sting coming up. But it sat there cleaned its wings, then just flew away, much to my relief. It wasn't till the evening when I was telling some friends about it that I had a thought, hang on was that a message for me. So, I went and got my totem book, and yes guess what it said – *It said stop moaning.* No, it didn't really, but what it did say and it resonated with me it was – *whatever task is upon you, jump in and go for it with enthusiasm and determination. Break out of your routine and do something adventurous.* After I read this, it made sense and I changed my thoughts about the trip, and actually I had a great time. But it took a wasp to tell me that. Now you may consider that it is just a coincidence and that all this is rubbish. However, the mystics have been using this for thousands of years and they take notes of the teachings and lessons being shown to them. I have to say that the above and all the messages I have received over the years are spot on to that thing I need help with at that time. This works and all because now I listen to what nature is telling me through the messages that she sends. This is another thought that what if it's not nature and it's my spirit guide or a loved one that has passed using nature to communicate with me. That is interesting in that, if that maybe true then the subconsciousness of those that have passed, and we will cover this in a bit more detail later, but those that have passed and my spirit guides are using nature to communicate with me, which is proof, to me at least, that we are connected to nature in a way that we don't understand fully at this time. I will leave that there, but if you are interested in getting a totem animal book, which I do recommend you do, then the one I use is by Steven D Farmer, PHD. It's titled *Animal Spirit Guides*. I am sure he won't mind me mentioning it, as it is a great no nonsense guide to the animals and insects that maybe trying to interact with you at any given time.

We will close this chapter with a thought. Nature affects us as we have seen every day, but what affect do we have on nature every day? Nature is a delicate being, but she is also a very powerful being. We, at times, abuse this delicate balance of nature with our thirst for things like timber and natural resources. There are some excellent programs in place that is planting as many trees as being harvested. But, as trees take away carbon dioxide and replace it by oxygen, we need trees. We need that balance, that part of nature that restores harmony. If we take too much without giving back, she will respond, and in a way that we have seen is not pretty with 'natural disasters' like earthquakes and obscure and unusual weather, tornados and heat waves. I said this wasn't going to be a sermon on climate change. Common sense will hopefully prevail that we need to give back as much as we take. But for us reading this book, for now go into nature see her and sense her and let her move into your busy lives by simply breathing in fresh air take note of the seasons and watch the wildlife around you, it will bring its rewards and feeling a part of something like nature, will allow that connective energy to come so that you realise you are not alone in this vast planet we live on. In fact, meditate in the open, find somewhere quiet and peaceful, close your eyes and just be in the moment, you may be amazed at actually how noisy nature is. Then open your mind to the messages brought to you by the use of nature, which come courtesy of the animals and insects around you. These messages are from a higher source that one day we will understand, but right now get yourself an animal totem book and just be alert with what is around you at the present time and then use your book to help decipher those messages. Take time to connect to the insects the wind and the birds, you see nature is alive and living, just allow it to flow and allow her energy to move through and within you.

There is one more point before I close of this chapter, and it is a personal note that I will leave with you. We think that we can control this planet we are on; we think that we take care of it and have worldly meetings to discuss how we can take care of her. We are so wrong; she can take care of herself as she has been doing for over three thousand million years. There will be a point that she will stamp her authority on the world, but I believe our biggest issues to us is the threat to ourselves. As mentioned, nature will take care of herself, she will always find a way. Nature doesn't need us to survive, but we do need her to survive, and the idea that we are in control is laughable.

Treat nature with respect and she will provide but treat ourselves with contempt and we won't.

We don't have three thousand billion years of experience in fact very little when you see how long we have been here compared to nature. Things like plants, bacteria and fungi do very well and do not need humans, humans need humans to survive. We may bring about our own demise and cause our own destruction due to our culture and ignorance of the planet we live on, and you know what? Nature will just carry on regardless. Sorry, a bit hard hitting but we have to realise that we need to take care of our home, as nature will step in to protect herself but she won't step into protect us only we can do that.

Chapter Three
Invisible Energy

Okay so we have looked at nature and the part where I say, feel connected to it, but how would you do that? The simple answer is that you are already connected to it and always will be connected to it. All you need to do, as we have covered, is to open up your mind that you are a part of this amazing world and are joined to it. We are all a part of this through that invisible quantum energy soup that connects everything to everything. Sound a bit strange, eh? We already believe the things we cannot see, i.e. Radio waves, we cannot see them, but they help us communicate and you know they are there as it produces sound. Light and electric again you cannot see it but it's there and you can observe the results of them being there. So, I get that when I say the invisible life force of energy and you say yea, show me. Well, I will try, but it's probably better for me to say that just because it's there and you cannot see it, doesn't mean it doesn't exist. Let's cover that again as it's important, radio waves, light and electric it's all there, all you need to do is see the results of its existence. When you are at home or work, listening to the radio, what are you doing? You are listening to radio waves, can you see or smell the source of it? No, but you know it's there as you are able to hear things around you. When you look around, you see the colours, shades and the light and dark. Do you notice that image coming toward you, can you actually see what you are observing? No. But you see the results as images are reflected through your eyes and into the brain in order for our brains to make sense of what we are seeing. In a thunderstorm you can, at times, feel the magnetic/electric atoms in the air dance and play. Do you see them no, you can see the results of them being there and can sense them and feel them around your body. Don't dismiss what you cannot see, hear, touch, taste or smell, just because you cannot use those senses to explain something, it doesn't mean it does not exist.

Let's start with the spiritual meaning then we can move onto the science behind it. You are made of, let's call it, conscious energy which originates from your conscient soul. This energy originates in that non-physical realm and is connected to the physical body. It can be seen at work through the physical body and the non-physical mind. Not to get this confused with the other energies the electric, light and sound which are non-living elements, we are in fact talking about that non-local energy. With me so far? Stick with it, it will make sense shortly. This energy is the life force that will enable us to keep moving forward and is existing in this world and nature, in fact all the elements we find around us. Why though do I say that electric and light are non-living? Simply that they are made either by us or through atoms interconnecting, which we will cover in the scientific segment, as I feel it's important to look at both points of view. This energy part I am talking about at this time, is the part that is us, it is not man made it purely exists as science is discovering. Remember the water experiment we first covered in the first chapter done by Dr Masaru Emote, where mere thoughts were projected onto water and in doing so changed their molecular structure? Well, that is the energy I am speaking about at this point. It's interesting to note that this non-local energy had an effect on the physical water. Shows how powerful it is and how it can be used for good and in some cases for the not so good. Like it or not we are spiritual beings and that brings with it spiritual energy. Now this doesn't matter in what religion or non-religious beliefs you have, as this energy is the manifestation of pure love that binds the soul to the physical body. And as such has to be everlasting. Yes, I know sounding a bit 'out there' again, but science is now catching onto this which we can look at a little later. And I am just telling this as it is, I am not a new world romantic and I don't dance around Stonehenge naked, well may be when I was younger but not at my age now. I am simply interested in looking at the world around me trying to understand it and by doing so living a better life for it. This information I am passing on is for you to make of it what you will. Yes, I am a medium and psychic, which is becoming more and more evident in a lot more people than it ever used to be. So, keep that mind open and your intrigue fresh and fluid.

Being connected or having an enlightenment period of your life, has been covered for hundreds of years by different religions and spiritual groups. The North American Indians saw this energy through the seasons and the four elements of the Earth and called it 'Mother Earth Spirituality'.

The Chinese called this energy 'Chi' and believe in a balance of yin and yang. Yin being the female and Yang being the male. Some also see that in light and dark, or indeed chaos and order. In other words, you have to have a balance between two competing energies. Asian religions and in particularly the Hindu have *Prana* which breaks down into a meaning of cosmic energy, or life sustaining energy. They believe that *Prana* resides in all living things and lives on after the death. They also have a belief that *Prana* comes back through reincarnation. Christian beliefs have a 'divine love' and energy that originates from God but yet is constant within us and around us. As you can see this non-local energy has had a place in our lives for hundreds of years and has been understood, or at least believed, by many albeit in various forms. The main point here is that it is believed to exist and even worshiped by many. Now I am not a type to be swayed by any beliefs, but as a practicing psychic I have seen this energy and felt it, which you can also do. For me, it's also interesting that the Hindu '*Prana*' belief also stands for breath, which means they also believe that perhaps we take in this energy every time we breathe so it's also a physical energy as well as a spiritual one.

Spiritual energy derives from the divine and take divine in whatever way you would like. But it is that energy we bring with us when we are born and to which we carry around with us, as it ebbs and flows through us every second of every day, month and year until we pass away.

Even then, it comes with us, as we move into the next world, realm or whichever way you want to look at it, it is a part of us and can manipulate water molecules, so it's much more powerful than we can imagine at this point in our lives, and must come from a source that is also more powerful than we know. Interesting thought, eh? That we are all part of something much more powerful than just us. This energy is around us, moves with us and is most prominent in nature and all that you see around you.

How do we feel or sense, this energy and connectedness? We first need to understand that we see the world around us in a 'reality' that has grown as we have matured. As, face it, when you were born you knew all about the non-local, even though our physical senses were being developed the day we came into this world, but we knew about non-physical domain before we let the 'outside' world into our being. What happens then is we let the reality of this world enter into our everyday lives and we lose the knack of being able to tap into and feel this natural energy around us. However, it is there and we know this because at times you will allow it into your psyche in the form of having things like gut feelings or reactions to events that happen spontaneously, intuition, dream states, premonitions and such things as times in your life that seen to follow a synchronistic pattern.

At the time these may seem disconnected to your normal 'reality' mind set. You may say things like, "That's strange, I feel I have done this before," or a Deja vu moment. Perhaps you have had a dream about something and a few days later that dream has manifested, possibly not in the way you dreamed, but it some way it correlates to that dream. What is happening during that time is you are allowing that energy come to you through the subconscious, which by the way helps control the way the natural energy comes to you, which then allows your conscious mind to work with it to enable you to have these insights or images etc. This non-local or invisible energy is not connected to what we think reality is, as reality at any time in your life is a product of space and time, which is what we need to navigate through our modern lives. This space and time is a man-made model to which we use at that point to help us gauge our lives through that part of our evolution as human beings. Gosh! That was a bit deep, wasn't it? So, let's try and break it down a little further. What I am trying to explain here, as best I can, is; we are connected to everything as our subconscious and our consciousness are not bound by this space and time reality we live by. We are more than just this carbon being as we covered earlier, without a spirit the mind and body are just parts of our human existence waiting to be engaged. With that spirit it all becomes joined and then things start to make sense. But, that spirit resides in the non-local space and our minds and bodies reside in this space, this reality, so in essence we need that non-local spirit to fuel what we perceive to do or be in this life through a mind and body experience. Our psyche then is connected to a space outside of the physical through the spirit. We just need to remember this and allow yourself to tap into that part of you, that at most part, is driving us but we don't give it the recognition or connect to it, which will give us a greater life experience and give us more of those Deja vu or spontaneous moments we look for in our everyday existences. Ah just one simple point before we move onto the scientific part of this. The North American tribes had a simple way of connecting into the Spirit of Mother Earth. All you have to do is to tap into each of the four elements and this was done so simply, but so powerfully for instance, if you want to tap and connect with the energy of the air, just turn your face into the wind or a breeze and close your eyes, open your mind and just feel that force on your face and body, don't think of anything except that energy flowing over you. Then let your senses guide you to thoughts of peace and tranquillity that comes into your mind. That's all you need to do, simple isn't it? Likewise, for water, prior to drinking it, pour some water into a glass and give thanks to that water for the life-giving qualities it will give you. Don't forget you can change the molecules of water by sending it positive thoughts and if that glass of water is positively charged, it may positively charge your body. As you can see, these are not complicated practices but will have a profound and positive effect on your being as you connect to the elements and in particularly your psyche, allowing that non-local energy to come to you, as you open up to it.

Okay I have bombarded you about this enough to give you some thoughts and brain matter on the subject, but to back up this 'spiritual side' to this non-local energy, what does science say about it?

Science can be complex so l will try my best to make it as simple as possible so we can all understand this complicated topic. To start, there is an extract from a science text: Physicists use the term nonlocal to describe the distant interactions of subatomic particles such as electrons. We can experience nonlocal mind spontaneously, paradoxically, without losing our individuality. A creator can live in many universes instead of simply adhering to a prescribed worldview such as the outmoded causal paradigm or unscientific beliefs. Again, I will try to make this read so that you understand the, at times, very complicated quantum theories. Basically, as quantum properties have characteristic randomness, connections between two or more things are typically revealed in averages of many measurements. The thing is that quantum mechanics insist that these properties are not fixed until they are measured which is how they know it/they exists. What this means is that a measurement on say a photon will instantly have an effect on the other photon across space. Okay, yes, a little complicated, let me try again. We know that every object is made of molecules and that these molecules are made up of smaller units called atoms. Now the book, or tablet you are reading this on, or the chair or table top you are sitting or leaning on is made up of atoms that because they are so tiny, we cannot see them. Here comes the interesting part, atoms are made up of subatomic particles, which have no real substance and instead are made up of energy waves. The same energy we looked at in the spiritual part. Yes, it's possible they are, and that makes me very interested, in as much as that in modern quantum mechanics they are studying and scientifically looking at the same thing that our subconscious minds are working with. As these subatomic particles are controlled by a nonphysical presence, then the spiritual and quantum science are actually looking at the same thing and that resides in the nonlocal form. The difference is that the spiritual person can sense it and see it in nature, whereas the science part is looking at this existence from a laboratory basis. It proves that there is a force of energy that is in nature and all around us, that both sides can detect, one naturally and one from a science point of view.

So, let's look a little deeper, as I feel this may explain a bit more, revert back to the part we mentioned above about things being made of atoms which in turn are constructed from subatomic particles. Science shows that we are made, (well in fact everything you see), is made of different parts of energy, or subatomic particles that vibrate at various frequencies, which produce the different things we see and feel from the chair you sit on, to grass, to rocks, to the clouds etc. But how do they seem solid? They seem solid as the physical brain works too slowly to see this energy field. It only sees and perceives from the physical nonlocal field, where the consciousness makes sense of what it sees and thus things appear solid. Whereas if we could see things from a subconscious point of view, where we don't have any limitation on the physical world and which is part of the quantum energy field, we would then be able to see things as pure energy AND of pure potential. This is where I believe those with the 'gift' can operate from, as they can connect with the subconscious and see this energy for what it is and what it can bring, and that there is a connection to nature. Let's face it our spirit is nothing more than pure energy which lays within our physical selves. It's our spiritual selves having that human experience. What happens if our spirit energy and that of all humans, animals, flowers the air, clouds etc. is all spiritual energy producing these energy particles. That means that we as a collective whole can manipulate these particles for good or bad. Amazing thought that if you had a group of 50 people in a room and 40 of those people had negative thoughts, how that would affect the area they are in and thus the other 10 people in that room. Tests have proved that those 40 people can have a dramatic effect on the rest of the group, which is similar to the water molecule exercise we read about earlier. Another way to look at this, remember when you walk into a church or cathedral how calm and peaceful it is? Well, that is due to the years of visiting parishioners that are giving off calming and peaceful energy to the surrounding area. The walls and the church capture this energy and it becomes a part of that building, so that when we walk into that area, we immediately pick up this energy. Same for when you walk into an old mansion or house, you can pick up the energy of all those years of occupation from its previous inhabitants. Sometimes you feel at ease and sometimes you can feel a little on edge. All you are doing is picking up the energy that is being held within the area or walls of that building you are in. Interesting, eh? That you are engaging with this energy field, or the effects of it without even trying. Imagine if you will, that if two thirds of the world's population were angry and upset, would it affect the rest of us? It is possible it would. Not only that, but as these negative thoughts resonate through the nonlocal energy super-highway, this negativity may affect everything around us, plants animals and the planet in general. Not sure if that's an interesting or depressing thought. As we are connected to nature and nature to us, perhaps we are having a more detrimental cause and effect on the planet than we realise, especially if we are finding life a struggle and are full of anger or we are stressed etc. The list is long. Wow! That's a worrying idea and not sure we should ponder on that for too long, or perhaps we should?

When we look back through history, it's interesting to note that during times of the 60s with its growing hippy and flower power culture, the world took on a happier guise. Likewise, during world crisis, things like the cold war and threat of nuclear war, the world was troubled and the worries of the masses had an effect on everyone, even those not directly affected. Not great examples perhaps, the point I am making is, if the majority of the populous is happy then that effect will cross over to the rest. Equally, if the majority are worried or stressed then that will affect the rest. It has to as we are part of and connected to each other and everything around us so unless you are strong and can connect to nature then you will let the worries and indeed happiness of others affect you and you wouldn't even realise that was happening.

So, to recap as I think this is important to grasp. Years ago, this had no substance, but science is now finding there is a connection at a subatomic level and perhaps even lower than that.

As we make more sophisticated instruments and places like the CERN accelerator, we are learning more about the world around our world and as a result discovering more about who we are. Perhaps a few hundred years ago, maybe not even as long ago as that, people that could 'talk to dead people' and connect with nature were burned at the stake. Maybe now as we learn more about who we are the practice of mediumship may become encouraged as we realise that all mediums and psychics are merely people that can connect to this invisible energy and work with, that energy. When the mind is capable of letting go of its rational state, it can enter a state where it may be able to perceive the physical and spiritual parts, where chaos and order abide, as both are necessary to survive and grow. We need to understand that both are required just like the Yin and Yang we need the female and male parts of us. Remember planet Earth originated from chaos when the big bang happened. I am not saying you need to have chaos in your life, but sometimes the bad, or unwelcome parts of our life happen to make way for the good part to happen. Which we covered in my previous book.

Our spirit then is what we should be connecting with, which will connect us to and is a part of that nonlocal domain. It is much more powerful than we ever imagined and connecting with it may make things more accessible to our limited conscious minds. That's why we should take time in nature to connect with this higher self. For hundreds of years scientists have been looking for but not quite finding, that elusive 'theory of everything'. All that looking has determined one thing and that is we are now understanding what we don't know. However, what has evolved from this science is that it has proven the existence of this nonlocal domain. Here comes the fascinating part, science states that this nonlocal, or non-locality theory explains how each of us is a shard of the holographic universe, that we are all capable of accessing all the information that is out there, if we could only tap into that particular frequency of our subconsciousness. Perhaps some of us can and are already doing that, for the rest, well as we have already mentioned, this nonlocal connection can be felt through the many facets and domains of nature that lives and moves around us.

Before we move on, let's see what we covered in this chapter. This world we are in is actually a result of being projected from the nonlocal domain where the 'spirit' truly lays. It can be felt and seen through nature if we only take the time to connect to it, as if we do then we will experience that incredible power, wisdom and understanding that we are trying to seek. Science is on the right path and is making amazing inroads, but I don't think we will ever truly know it all, as after all, we need some mystery about our existence as what else would we gossip and ponder about. Being in nature, and that can be a simple walk in the woods or over a meadow or perhaps by the sea, will help us connect if we can close our minds to the physical and open to the natural. My concern is that if we take too much from our planet without putting back, we are shutting out our spiritual selves from having that greater understanding and experience. As already stated, this is not a sermon on saving the planet but common sense says that if we take too much then we are killing off the physical which our spiritual selves need in order to evolve and grow. The ancients all over the planet used to connect and understand that an invisible part of the universe existed, we lost that during time, but science is now beginning to acknowledge and comprehend that there is a nonlocal domain and that we, as humans, connect not only to each other but to everything else on this physical world we call Earth. I will leave you with that thought as we move onto the next chapter.

Chapter Four
Life of Meaning

As we have covered nature and the invisible world, it leads on to looking at the existence of life, or rather the meaning of life as we perceive it. Actually, perhaps we should turn it around and look at a 'life of meaning'. Why? As I think that if we understand nature and what's behind nature and us, as human beings, then it leads onto why we are here and what that meaning of life signifies. Philosophers have been pondering over those words for centuries as have I, although obviously not for centuries. I also think at some stage you have to, as we are humans and as such, I think it's our right to ask that question from time to time.

The existence of life can mean different things to different people. It can be a syntactic ambiguity which means a sentence can have one or two meanings. Are we looking at the existence of life i.e. life forms, or our existence of life? And of course, I mean the latter. Our existence of life and, what does it mean for us? The basis of this question is that we are born, we live through the middle part and then we die. I started asking myself questions around this middle part long ago when I was a small boy. One day, on the way back from my grandma's, I asked my wonderful dad, "So as Grandma is now old," as tact was never a strong point for me, "when she dies, would she have been happy with her life?" You can tell that even at a young age I was a little strange. My dad looked at me and said, "Why do you ask that?"

I said I was scared that when I get to Grandma's age how would I know I have lived a good life. My dad looked at me a little perplexed and said because you would have lived your life, and if you can live your life, I am sure that it will have made you happy. That answer scared me, if I lived my life, I will be happy. How do I live my life? Yes sure, I would finish school, get a job, get married have children, get a mortgage and trudge to work in the morning and home in the evening. Get into a little debt look at what I can afford to buy and drool over that Ferrari I can't afford to buy. Sounds depressing doesn't it? But to a 10-year-old looking at my life ahead, that's what it looked like, as that was entering my mind at that age when I watched the news and listen to the grown-ups around me. Were they happy? Yes, they seem to be, but maybe there was a distant longing in their eyes looking at a faraway horizon in search for the meaning they seemed to be looking for, and that question, that question we all ask ourselves at times, that 'is this it' question. At the same time, I started thinking about my own immortality, is there really a God, is there really a place called heaven? Yes, my gift allowed me insights into other worlds, but to a 10-year-old that was confusing rather than helping. Could I really achieve anything I set my mind to? What is death? And what if I died without living that life I wanted rather than that life which seemed to be preordained. Then I thought more about God, I asked my parents and teachers, "This person we call God, can I read about him?" So they gave me a bible. I read some of it, but it still didn't answer the questions I needed answering. I continued to ask that if this God person really existed and that if we really knew he existed by some means, what would it do for me? What would it do for humankind? I will stop here and say, this isn't an attack on any kind of religion, just me as a small boy trying to find my way and asking questions some didn't or don't like to ask. If we saw God and He came to us, not in the guise of anyone else, but himself, would that change people's perceptions about life? Would it change our thoughts on living a meaningful life, or a life full of meaning? It may change our perceptions about what life is and make us in some way more hopeful, but fundamentally what would change? Okay, a bit deep and meaningful but ask yourself that question, if that question you really wanted to know about life came from a higher source, would it really change your life? Or would it simply send you on another quest as the answer you got fired off yet more thoughts and ideas about life and your part in it?

What does **meaning** mean? A life of meaning or the meaning of life, but what does meaning actually mean? Philosophers state that meaning is a relationship between two sorts of substances.

Which are signs and the kinds of things these signs bring. Augustine states, a sign is 'something that shows itself to the senses and something other than itself to the mind'. Let's look at that a little closer as I think he has something there. Something that shows itself to the senses, means that something is in the here and now you can use your senses to hear, touch, taste, see or smell it. That part is okay, and I understand that, but it's the hidden meaning in the next part I like the 'other than itself'. So that means that thing that we use our senses to understand is not what we think it is. Then the last part 'to the mind'. The mind, that's us what we are perceiving at any given point in time. Put that context to our meaning of life, and then rethink that phrase above, so the meaning of life perhaps is **'something other than itself to the mind'**. Does that mean that the traditional way of looking at our meaning of life and our place in it is a little squiffy, perhaps we are looking in the wrong place? If life is something other than itself to us, then what is it? This 'other than itself' surely means it's not what we think it is, it's more than itself to our minds, to us. If we are the physical, then the 'other' must be the spiritual 'thing' we are looking for. If we are the physical in the here and now, then perhaps, we are looking too closely to the physical parts of our being here on this planet and missing the spiritual part. That other part to our being we forget as we live too closely by using our here and now, those five senses. Interesting, isn't it? That maybe a lot to what we seek on this earth is hidden in plain sight. It's there all we need to do is open our minds to seeing what is there. In other words, **we don't see things as they are, we see things only as we see.**

Do we try to understand things by putting too much logic into it and make things too complex? As I discussed in my first book, nature isn't complicated we only make it complicated by trying to fathom the obvious, that thing that is right in front of our eyes. So, why do we do that? I think because we/most of us live from the mind that logical part of our being, instead of living from the heart. Living from the heart sounds a little flower power I know, but believe me it's more than that, and if done correctly it connects you to the wider nature. Sometimes logic just doesn't roll, it becomes too complicated and two-dimensional. Allowing yourself to emerge within nature through letting yourself simply love will open up doors and things suddenly make sense it becomes clear and common sense comes to your aid. If you want to know the reason why you and everything exists, just take time to stop, be still and quiet, open your mind to the fact that you are connected, as we saw in chapter three. Then allow your heart to beat, listen to it, feel it and allow your mind to acknowledge its existence. Breathe deeply and allow your chest to expand with every breath, then let go and allow yourself that luxury of feeling that positive energy and calm enter your very being. That positive charged energy you get when you open yourself up to nature is what breathes life into every living thing on the planet. There is likely some kind of chemical or mathematical equation for this positive energy, but for now let's just call it love.

We have seen what the 'meaning' part of this equation maybe our spiritual selves, so now let's look at the second part the 'of' in Meaning **of** Life. What is of? In some scripture and titles the 'of' is small and not very important, which I feel is not a true representation of this little word, and for us in this chapter this word has a deeper meaning. 'Of' as per the dictionary, is the relationship between the part and the whole, or between a scale or measure and a value. What does that mean here? Meaning of life or a life of meaning. We have seen that 'meaning' can also signify a sign, or a way forward remember it's 'something other than itself' so perhaps this little **of** being the relationship between meaning and life is the missing part.

It may mean that the 'something other than itself' which we know is our spiritual selves plus now the of which we have seen can be a 'part or value' which may look like the following.

Meaning = Our Spiritual selves
Of = being a part or value of
Okay, adding those two parts together says, **our spiritual selves are a part or has value** to? Well, the next part is our life. Let's then look at what life actually means.

Life has many connotations it can mean, reproduction, activity, birth or even death etc. There is, however, another description and that is growth. Life of course means living and as we live, we grow. First of all, physically, from a small boy or girl into a man or woman, but perhaps it's also about our spiritual growth, or as I mentioned earlier, what we do in between our birth and death. Of course, we all have different ideas about how we should be living our lives in-between birth and death. Growth then, let's look closer at this area. We know that there is a physical part to growth, but there is also the spiritual part and it's this basis that I want to cover here. Yes, I can hear you groan and say here he goes again but keep with me. We are all searching for something in this life, a better understanding or a skill, perhaps a way of living but I think most of us, and especially in modern life, are all looking for that connection. We are aware that there is more to what we do in this physical life of ours, and I think this leads on to what we are missing which may be our spiritual or conscious growth, and if we are honest, I believe we all look to understand this from time to time. Spiritual or conscious growth is simply understanding that there is another part to our being, as we covered in the previous chapters. Fact, we are all connected to each other in every aspect of our being, which in turn means we are affected at a conscious level by the outside world. Fact, the thoughts and feeling of others can have an effect on us as individuals as the collective consciousness of the whole is affected by the majority. Fact, you can break away from letting these thoughts affect you if you realise you are part of this process and have the ability to be you. How then, do we achieve this spiritual growth? This can be achieved by the simple act of becoming one with the world around you, BUT also rejecting the consciousness of the masses, which can be achieved by taking responsibility for your own actions, having patience, taking time to be in harmony with the natural world around you, being compassionate and above all living in a state of love. Easier said than done isn't it? Especially when the media keeps reporting on the bad things that happen in our world. Sure, it is, but remember, that's the job of the media to inform on such things, not many newspapers will be sold if the papers were all about nice things. That's a shame about our world as it is, people buy papers to read about this so-called reality we live in. Is it? Is it really the reality we live in or just the world we create through its mishaps and misunderstandings that the media may fuel, with its efforts to create stories for the masses to read. As I mentioned above, the masses create these uneasy feelings we sometimes experience, through the invisible connections we all have. You see life isn't complicated, if we just understand that to have the life, or growth we seek we just need to step back and look at the wonderful world around us, which becomes stronger when we connect to nature. Yes, understand that the world has these moments of madness, but also be aware you don't need to be a part of it. Through love for the world around you and taking responsibility for you, for what you do, means you can break away from this conscious thinking and just be you.

Meaning of life then we have seen that:

Meaning = Our Spiritual selves
Of = Being a part or value of
Life = Growth

The meaning of life then is our 'spiritual selves being a part of or value of our growth', or the other way around a life of meaning means 'growth being a part of or a value to our spiritual selves'. Whichever way you look at it, it basically means that in order to grow we need to recognise we have a spiritual part of us that requires to be fed in order to grow. If we allow that to happen, we grow within this life, and if we grow, our spiritual selves develop and that will give us that all-important meaning, as like most things, if you feed something it grows and become stronger. i.e. give a young seedling some earth to live in, give it water, some sun and it grows strong and true, becoming what it is meant to be. So simple isn't it? Just like us, but as we have a thinking mind, we also need to stimulate this, which we will cover in the next chapter.

Okay, the meaning of life is to stimulate our spiritual selves in order for it to grow and thus in doing so it allows us, our conscious selves to develop. How then do we allow our spiritual selves to grow in order to feel that connection to nature and more importantly, for us, as individuals on this earth to become more empowered? As we have covered, we are part of a collective whole, but also, we have a **core self**, as I like to call it. A self that although is connected, is a part of you as an individual, which allows you to be who you are. Your thinking mind is different to those around you as is your DNA, it allows you to function differently to everyone else. It's this part of our 'personal' selves that we need to develop. Being part of a collective whole doesn't mean we need to act the same as everyone else or need to have the same outlooks and perspectives.

We are all feeding this wholeness through our experiences, and unless we start to push ourselves as an individual, we will become lemmings and maybe humanity will start to look totally process driven and growth will be slow and starved, which is something we don't want especially for future generations. Our core self needs to grow, we simply cannot compare ourselves to others around us. We all have a different path to walk and different experiences to encounter. If you begin to open your mind and heart to these experiences, then you are allowing that growth and your meaning of life will start to reveal itself to you. Patience is the key here as is walking and experimenting on your strengths and weaknesses. As mentioned above, taking responsibility for your actions means opening your mind and heart to trying different things, and if they fail then always remember, **'there is no such thing as failure only feedback'**, which I also covered in my first book. In other words, push yourself, try different things and if it doesn't work, then there is a reason. Doing this will begin to open your heart and mind to the path you are either walking on, or realising you need to walk a different one. All that is needed is a little trial, error and patience. When I look back at my life to date, I tried so many different things to become that top boardroom executive and interestingly, the closer I became, the more I realised it wasn't for me.

That's not to say it won't be for others, just not for me. It was during one of the meetings I attended that I noticed most of my colleagues were happy being led, as I tried to push a point home during a meeting that met with disapproval. It was after the meeting my manager, who was also present, took me to one side and said, "I really like your idea."

I said, "So, why didn't you back me?"

And he said, "In front of all the others? I don't think so, I don't want to look like an idiot." And with that, he walked away.

A lemming moment that made me sit up and take note that the boardroom, for that particular company, had given up to walking the same path as the rest. I recognised that there has to be a leadership format, but a company that listens to all levels of the organisation will grow, one that follows a directive from the top like lemmings will eventually fail as there is no fluidity to the organisation. I digress, it was just an example that if we follow the crowd then there will be no personal growth and if there is no personal growth then our individual meanings of life will get confused and be swallowed up with the masses.

Another helping point here to discover your meaning or growth of the spiritual self is to become aware of the present moment. Too much searching for meaning may increase tension and confusion and lead to inner conflict, as the answers you are looking for may become lost or obscured. The first lesson for discovering your growth is to remain in the here and now, in other words the present moment. Not easy if you don't have patience, which is why first practicing patient is very important, not easy in this fast-paced world we live in. I was at the back of the queue when they gave out patience, but practice makes perfect and I for one am a lot more patient and tolerant than I ever used to be which allows me to be in, and to enjoy, the power and grace of what being in the present moment brings. The second idea to help you find meaning is to accept who you are at any given moment. Yes, sure we will have good times bad times laughs and 'cries. This is all part of growing, remember you are a spirit having a human experience so learn to let go and just become the person you are. Don't follow the crowd, dare to be different as you push the boundaries of who you are. If you learn to accept that if you are reading this then you are human and in the here and now, then allow those unique imperfections to surface, recognise them as you, acknowledge them and then change the ones you can, the ones you cannot will be simply be a part of who you are. You are as unique and just as amazing as the person next to you, who will have their own imperfections and will learn that these differences are just a part of them. These are not weaknesses, on the contrary they can be seen as your strengths. Why strengths? Because you will have to learn to accept them, and in doing so it will increase that inner strength. Why is an inner strength important? Because that inner strength is part of our core self, that self which is important as you allow yourself to grow and learn. It is that part of us that doesn't live in material wealth, it doesn't live in the media tittle tattle of you are supposed to do this, or don't do that, eat this and don't drink that mentality. It doesn't need to live there as it already knows what is good for it, for us, if you learn to listen. As the Dalai Lama states, *'If you find a deep and profound love for the inner being, you will start to live within, and if you can do that you will never be without.'* In other words, have that deep inner love for yourself, your imperfections and your strengths just be prepared to push the boundaries a little and become you. Sure, we will all have moments, tantrums, anger, frustrations, but recognise these as growth patterns that need to be understood not run away from, and don't hide them by pushing them deep into your psyche. Just take time to appreciate why, then dismiss them as a moment in time that will have a lesson to learn which will add to your future growth as a spiritual being in this human world.

All sounds all a bit 'out there', doesn't it? But it's similar principles to the greats of the past, Einstein, De Vinci, Aristotle, Plato, Socrates, Dalai Lama, Hypatia and even closer to home with Churchill, all had an idea of the above and worked to understand themselves using these principles. It's not rocket science and to me it makes sense, if you are going to have this meaning of life moment, or as we have seen '*growth giving value to our spiritual self*' then you need to push the boundaries of what you think is normal and allow yourself to have a spiritual moment and practice the above. I am just a normal guy that simply wants to learn more about who we/I am. I don't practice strange rituals, I don't go to church very often, I don't eat a strange diet. I go to football, I swear, I frequent the local pub and occasionally I will have a cigarette. Ah gosh shame, I smoke now and again! And I have the ability to speak to dead people. But these are my experiences while here living this human life. As long as I am not hurting anyone else and I continually respect people, then I shall continue 'living' this existence. If all that is a little shocking, you will get over it as you realise these are my imperfections, as I am positive you will have some of your own, which is just a sign that you are having a 'human' experience.

In this chapter, we have seen that perhaps that meaning of life we seek is in fact growing our spiritual selves, which in turn will help our inner selves to grow. If we learn to listen to the inner you, not the world around you and walk your own path, you will become that individual. Practice being in the moment, by being quiet, reflective and at peace. Accept yourself for who you are, stop trying to be that 'other' person. Recognise you are totally unique to the person next to you and accept your imperfections no matter how small or large they may be, it's part of this growth we encounter on this planet, it is a part of who you are, and above all it's just YOU. Be you and the world and everyone in it will accept you for what you are. If you try to be something you are not, you send out confusing signals to not only those around you, but more importantly to yourself and that could cause negative inner dialogues to start which leads to insecurities and other mental issues to bubble up from within, and we don't want those. Okay, so we have had a look at that this meaning to your existence may actually mean, what's next and how does that fit into your world? Good question. Let's have a look.

Chapter Five
Your Life in This world

In the last chapter, we considered that this meaning we sometimes search for may be spiritual growth and not the physical part of our being. We saw our physical existence has an impact on our spiritual growth as we navigate through this human experience we are having in this life at this time.

As we navigate through this world and our life within it, most of us will have a view from our own point of awareness. We may consider that we are on our own and thus our existence is more important than the next person, that old dog eat dog situation. We strive to live for us as an individual, our growth is very much a unique experience as we need to learn for our own success and prosperity, as well as our life's experiences and our ups and downs, in whichever area that may be. Never forget that at the same time we are all connected, so this individual experience we require has to be balanced with the fact we are all connected to each other and to everything around us. How would we be able to achieve this balance? Simply that if you know what you really desire in this existence and start to pursue it, it then becomes personal to you. You can do this for anything you wish to achieve, be it a daily challenge, or to that one life changing decision and pursuit. Once you have this realisation of a desire or goal remember that there is the quantum soup all around you connecting you to all the energy and help that you may need to achieve this goal or desire. If we try to do anything in this life alone, at times we will fail as we may not have the necessary skills or knowledge to achieve what we want. If, however, you can access this quantum soup, you will have all the skills and knowledge around you to help you and things will become so much easier and achievable. It's like doing some research on a subject like the great battles of the Duke of Wellington and sitting in a bare room with nothing in it to help you, except your own imagination. How would you get on? Probably not very well and you may become frustrated, confused and anxious? Imagine you are doing this research in the national library in London, how easy would that research become? You would have everything around you needed to do this study, it would be straightforward and you wouldn't need to exert a great deal of effort. That's exactly what you need to do when embarking on a new idea, or desire, yes, it's your initial thought and idea, but then engage the universe around you to help bring that idea into fruition. If you are connected to all the resources you require, it will just be like sitting in that library.

I talk about using this energy, but how do you tap into it and use it? How do you use something you cannot touch, see or feel? You use that old-fashioned part of us that not many use to-day as technology gives us everything we could need. Or does it? Perhaps technology as discussed earlier is taking away that part of us needed to understand the world around us. The great thinkers of the past, the inventors and philosophers, painters and architects etc. all had two things in common when creating something, (which was long before computers were invented), they used common sense and instinct. Common sense we have covered, but what about instinct, I think, as a race we have forgotten how to use that instinct that our forefathers and mothers applied to create and understand the world around them. What does instinct actually mean? With instinct you have, those gut feelings which is the universe and subconscious talking to you. It's the subconscious part of you that recognises that you are connected to everything around you and so much more besides. It's that universal plug in you require in your daily life and in fact it is with you 24/7 it never switches off. Problem is, as mentioned, the more we rely on technology to solve our initial questions and struggles the more we move away from these instincts that will help us with the answers we seek. Let's revisit nature and see where instinct falls within that realm. Instinct within nature comes within a fixed pattern of behaviour to response or have responses to certain stimulus that an animal will find itself in. That animal will learn to survive its world by adapting certain behaviour when faced with a familiar situation, but it can and does adapt very quickly to changing situations and circumstances so that when faced with a different dilemma it learns and then installs a new behaviour which then becomes an instinctual part of its being. It is continually learning and adapting, changing and then developing new behaviours to new situations, which then becomes instinct, it's called instinctual behaviour. Why then are animals able to do that, where we as a race struggle to move and flow to new situations and develop those new instincts which connects us to that energy we need to learn from and develop as an individual? There may be many theories, but I believe we disconnect from learning new things as our culture behaviours limit us from really connecting. In my first book I mention that when we are born, we don't have fears or traits as we use instinct to find our way within the first few months of our lives. Where does that instinct come from? As a mother, you didn't feed the baby information or plug yourself in to a laptop so the unborn baby can download information. The baby is born and it immediately uses instinct to find its way around this new world. When we give a baby a new object to play and investigate, unless it's in a stroppy mood and throws it on the floor, it will look at that object, feel it, touch it, smell it and probably taste it. (Forgive me for using its. but I am trying to cross the his/hers divide). It is using its instincts to find out about that object in unison with its five senses to understand what it has been presented with. It will form an opinion about that object, a like or dislike, then it will file those findings away to be used again. But as he/she grows up, this instinctual behaviour will be replaced by allowing others' opinions and ideas to enter his/her minds. It allows technology to map out the world around them and then instinct becomes lost and forgotten as its dependency on what it hears, sees, or has been told, takes over. That's when I believe cultural differences sabotage us, as he/she starts entering a culture behaviour of the environment they find themselves in, which may develop their action fixed behaviour rather than an instinctual based behaviour. It's written that when a culture behaviour has been developed it replaces our natural instincts as we become too attached to education and where we deem our social standings are and the dependency of technology. We lose that ability to tap into that universal energy as we rely too much on information given to us. We forget how to use that nature, or energy, or part of our being, we forget how to use our senses, consciousness, common sense and instinct to help guide us. It is that instinct that got us, as human beings, to where we are now from time spent living in caves. But as the modern world and its trappings descend onto our lives more and more and technology becomes our partner in almost everything we do, we let go of our instincts our sense of being, we lose the knack of being able to work things out and allow that quantum energy into our lives. That's where we struggle to move forward and where we lose the ability to understand the natural, real world that is around us with all its power grace and beauty, that can and that tries to help us and guide us through every second of our lives. How do we get back into using and understanding those instincts that will allow us to become more fluid in our world?

Some people may get a little confused with the difference between instinct and intuition, so I think it's important at this stage to understand the variation. Instinct is a natural, inbred tendency toward a behaviour driven by your subconscious. Whereas intuition is a learned process through rational thoughts, that get filed away. To break it down instinct is a powerful behaviour driven natural process fuelled by the subconscious that takes on 17+million bits of information a second. Intuition, on the other hand, uses process driven behaviours taken from your experience on this Earth that uses smaller amounts of information, as the conscious part of the mind isn't as strong nor as fast as the subconscious part of the mind. Both can be used to make decisions as we move through life, but perhaps use the intuition to understand the issues and questions etc., but use those instincts to guide you through that behaviour needed to be certain of the outcome. One thing to remember, instinct may not necessarily give you the answer you may be looking for, as it might give you another question, which is fine, as what it is doing is making you look at that possible scenario from another point of view. If that happens, you are still on the right path, although we sometimes fail to see that if that question may seem like another obstacle. Stick with it, it's all the same process but there may be another lesson to be learnt before you find the answers you are looking for, remember it's only a 'tiger' so keep moving forward. How do we tap into those instinctual behaviours? First, you have to live in the moment and focus on the task you are doing at that moment, don't listen to your mind, it will try to take you away to another time or memory of thought, just try and stay in the present moment. We touched on this in chapter four. It takes time and practice, but believe me it works and it does centre you to the here and now. When you wake up and see the day ahead, stop and say to yourself, *"Today I will focus on the best I can for me."* Then let it go but try and stay in the present moment on anything you do during the day. This does work and it does bring results, it takes practice, but if you can crack it, gosh you will be totally blown away by the results. Stay away from fear, we covered fear in the first book so remember 'fear' doesn't exist, only in the part of the mind that it says it does. In other words, it's not real, it's only your mind tricking you into believing that something is fearful from using a past experience and using it in a present time scenario. If you stay in the present time and just say to yourself that this situation I am in now has never happened before nor will it ever happen again, so why am I using past experiences to tell me how to live now? Unfortunately, that's just the mind keeping you away from harm and taking you toward pleasure, by pointing out that this situation maybe worth avoiding. But how do we grow if we don't get a little out of our comfort zone? Meditation is a fantastic way to centre yourself in the here and now and allow that intuition to come through. It doesn't have to be for an hour a day, just being quiet and switching off for five or ten minutes or when you can. Allow yourself to centre and bring your thoughts to your breathing or listen to some soothing music, just let your mind be calm and it will also help bring that instinct to the forefront of your thoughts. Let your mind to be fluid and three-dimensional, remember get out of your comfort zone, take small chances and don't follow the crowd, as it is just possible that the crowd are also lost. Following people who are lost won't get you to where you want to be going. I had a great saying in my first book, '**Know the rules so you know how to break them**' – love that. What it means is know how your mind and life can sabotage you, then turn the tables and make life work for you. Finally trust, start to trust what comes to you, it may not be a huge light bulb moment and, to be honest, most instinct moments are not like that, they come to you subtly and quietly. You will know when they do as it fits, it feels right and takes no effort to follow, you just need to trust in those inner feelings and flow with it. It takes some practice as we are not programmed or taught to use instincts these days, so ignore modern day trappings and allow your mind to be quiet from time to time, allow that inner subconscious to speak to you. As mentioned, you will be amazed at what may come to you. Let's move on from instinct and look at another part of your life in this world.

One thing you will discover is that we/you still have a lot to live for in this life, at all times, no matter what the circumstances. We all need things at different times and at different stages of our lives, we all seek that existence that meaning and fulfilment in our lives. Things move at such a fast pace technology, work, our precious spare time, whatever that is, things are constantly changing and evolving. Trouble is, I think it evolves too quickly for us to keep up with as at times, I feel we get left behind. Look at aviation, modern planes are now so sophisticated they can basically outfly the pilots. Cars, I have so much technology in my car that I probably won't use half of it. I even have Wi-Fi in my car now, can you believe that? Only 20 years ago, we were getting the hang of fuel injection and not having to use a choke, now my car has Wi-Fi.

I'm finding I get myself in a little muddle trying to keep up with it all, but that's the problem with me and I think a lot of people, we don't actually need to know it all. Do we really need that latest bit of kit that will help us navigate around an obscure little island in the Indian Ocean, while I am sitting at home? All we need to know right now is your place within this ever-changing world. I feel sad when I look back at when I was growing up as a little boy, looking at this world in awe and wonder, and looking at the way some children are today, with the only wonder in their eyes is when their mobile phone or tablet shows that it's fully charged. I was very fortunate that my wonderful mum and dad would let me ask the strangest questions and not tell me to be quiet or dismiss me for asking those questions, in fact they encouraged me. They may not have had the answers, but my dear dad would go to the set of Britannica Encyclopaedia's we had on the shelf and have a look. If the answer was there, great, if not he would ask me what I thought the answer would be. He was encouraging my inquisitive mind to look for the answers. People of my age may remember those encyclopaedias on bookshelves at home or at school. Such amazing sources of information, they were in a set of about 10 or 12 volumes covering so many subjects. Perhaps that's the price of evolution we have forgotten how to look things up for reference or information, there is very little of the old traditions left of going to a library and then using your brain to search along the book shelves for that book, then looking to find what it is you were looking for within its pages. Now, it's Google, or other search engines, type in a word and hey presto, the answer is there. Doesn't take much effort, does it? So how do you fit in within this fast paced, incredibly technology driven world we live in? The Dalai Lama states: *I believe that the very purpose of life is to be happy. From the very core of our being, we desire contentment.* I can take that, if we continue to make those small in roads into what we desire, and we make those small but important steps listen to our instinct and allow ourselves to be in the present moment, then we will walk our individual paths and not those of others. We are then on the way to finding that contentment. Always remembering that we are individuals living in the quantum soup which means we are not alone in our quest for that thing we need to accomplish. What exactly is contentment? This may have different meanings to us all. According to the dictionary contentment means content, satisfaction, happiness gratification, peace, well-being. It is also having that all-important fulfilment in whatever it is you seek. Now for me that's the most important meaning to contentment. Let's have a little closer look at fulfilment, as when you are fulfilled it will not only bring contentment, it will also bring on that knowing of where your place is in this life. It will open up your being to other feelings of belonging and it will connect you to that higher source that most of us are seeking.

Having fulfilment is achieving that thing promised or required and that's the whole point of this book, it is to get you to look at your world from a different place, that place of understanding and a realisation that you have everything you need to obtain that thing you require. If you can continue to strive for what it is you desire and make that progress toward it, then you will find it will be a matter of when, not if. Fulfilment will also bring you peace, a deep feeling of peace that everything is on track and you are enjoying the journey. And, of course it will be on track and as you experience life's little up's and down's, these will be tolerated as you will be operating from a deeper place where everything you need will be right there for you to tap into. Fact is there is still a lot for you, us, to learn and remember you don't need to know everything at this moment. As you live from that contentment, which is brought on by working toward your desire and being fulfilled in what you do, then you will be able to accept life's little lessons for what they are, and that is simply a lesson to be learned. It doesn't have to be who you are; it doesn't have to be the new you, just a lesson to be understood, learned and then move on. Simple, isn't it? There is nothing complicated about our lives, only us, that makes things far too complicated at times.

I get told by some people, oh yes this is all well and good, but it isn't reality. Really? What exactly is reality? As per the dictionary, 'it's the state of things as they actually exist, as opposed to an idealistic or notional idea of them.' That's interesting, isn't it? It's the state of things as they actually exist. That important word there, as they **actually** exist, not in the way we think they exist. Actually, implies the thing that is there is real, it has substance. The quantum soup is there we know it's there as science has proven it to be there, we know it's real. So, that's the reality part so what's the 'opposed to an idealistic or notion idea of them'? That is the part of us that uses false information to navigate our world, including thinking that we are alone and separate from everything in the universe, instead of using that common sense and instinct. In essence when I get asked about the reality of this life, I say, reality is the part of this life we should be working or living from. Not from a misconstrued idea of what we think reality is, which is born from fear, lies and using false information given by well-intentioned people around us. That was a bit strong to which I apologise, but it does concern me when people are misled by others that live and work from these false ideas about how the rest of us should, or should not be doing in order to fulfil our lives. You see the reasonable person will try and adapt and mould himself to the world around him/herself, whereas the person that breaks away from normal thinking and being, will adapt the world to themselves thus having greater success. If you don't believe me, look at all the very well-off entrepreneurs, they saw a gap in the market or pushed themselves to change the way we buy or shop or work and by doing so have made themselves a lot of money. The flip side is the person that realises they want more from life from a similar point of view, who sold up and bought a small holding in the countryside. Break away from the normal and stop following the crowd as otherwise all you will be doing is living from the ideas of others. Stop adapting to others points of views and ideas and raise yourself above these people, see things for what they are, use that common sense, instinct and realise this is your spiritual growth not someone else's.

As we have seen, your life in this world is not complicated, it's not deep and it's not mystical, but it is yours to control or indeed not, as the case may be. One thing you do need is to tap into that one true source and let it enter your life. Using and understanding what comes from common sense and instinct will allow you to tap into that energy soup, which will help bring about your desires and that in turn will bring fulfilment in all you do. If you can bring fulfilment into your daily lives and routines, then it will bring about that peace of mind and body, and that is really what your life in this world is all about. It is not for others to control, it's not for others to dictate to you how you should live it. Just as important, it is also not for you to control others' lives, it is their life and they live it, yes at times frustratingly, but they live it their way. As long as you don't hurt anyone else in the process, go and live the life you desire, no matter what it is, as you have all the resources to hand if you just let it come to you. While writing this chapter it dawned on me that perhaps in order to continue this growth and to give you an overall understanding that we need to look at our consciousness. As we have seen we need to connect to nature, there is this quantum soup we are connected to, that invisible energy that binds everything in nature together. The meaning of life could be your personal spiritual growth, which is grown from within, not from without. And your life in this world means using those spiritual strengths of instinct and common sense to allow the greater voice to communicate and guide you. At this point, I think we need to look at our consciousness which may help to understand a little more about us.

Chapter Six
Birth of Consciousness

There has been a lot of deep and meaningful conversations about the conscious and some deep and meaningful books written on the subject. What I will try and do here is make it as light and as understanding as possible, as remember I don't like complicated. I will start with my own experience of why I believe there are two parts to us as human beings, those two parts being the subconscious and conscious. When I was a little boy, I always felt a little different to those around me. I already told you about the time I saw my dead uncle in the kitchen beside my mother, which at the time although scared me also seemed to be quite natural. Long after that particular episode, I questioned that perhaps we have two parts to us, that part which is the here and now, and that part which is separate to us as physical beings but is connecting us to a higher self. When I was at school, we were taught about our conscious and Darwin's theory of evolution. I understood what we were being taught, but it didn't really sit comfortably with me. I grasped the idea that an insect nest, let's say an ant, builds that nest the way they do as they don't really have another concept as to why, they just build them in that manner and, in effect they are not consciously aware of building a nest in any other way. In other words, there is no comprehension in the ant's world, or, there isn't a thinking brain no cognitive thinking, just a process kind of behaviour born from following a set of principles and actions which hasn't evolved for millions of years. Where we as humans have evolved and as such, proves that we have that cognitive ability or at least a comprehension which has evolved from our ability to think and form such ideas around language and culture. As our culture and language grew and took shape, so did our thoughts about the world we live in. I got that and it made sense. However, there was still something niggling at the back of my mind. It wasn't really until I was in my twenties when I had that realisation that there is two parts to us. That here and now conscious part of us but there had to be another part that was allowing me, and lots of others too, that ability to tap into another world or time in space. A bit Star Trekkie, eh? The conscious mind still helps, guides and gives us learnings from our culture behaviour's but, the subconscious also grows, not necessarily from our behaviours but from our time spent on and in this time on the earth. I believe it takes everything onboard about our personal and spiritual growth and uses that to give us an inner picture of the universe and our part in it. That's why I feel we need to tap into this more often and understand that the subconscious is far more powerful and understanding than our conscious minds. Let's discuss culture behaviour a little more as I feel it's important for you to recognise the reason why culture behaviour has an influence on our consciousness. We touched on this little in the previous chapter. Culture behaviour has to be taught it is not instinct, but it could be classed as intuitive. As we read earlier, intuitive thoughts have to be installed and learned and then gets filed away for future use, which matches what we believe culture behaviour is. So, culture behaviour is what we learn from our various beliefs and what we absorb as we grow and progress as a human race, how does that affect our consciousness? It affects our consciousness by what we learn, at this time and from times past. If our conscious is forever growing learning and developing, then we must be passing on this growth to our children and our children onto theirs and so on. Ancients had a conscious mind but was it advanced as ours is now? The answer must be no, and will our conscious mind be more advanced in another 500 years than it is now? The answer must be yes. It is continually adapting, evolving, growing and learning. What I find interesting is that over the last say, 1000 years our consciousness has expanded but the humble ant hasn't, and yet it is still thriving, growing and it is still in existence. What I am trying to highlight here is if the ant hasn't evolved from what it has been doing for thousands of years, and yet we supposedly have with our growing mind and awareness born from our culture behaviour, are we more advanced than the ant? Or are we simply keeping up with nature? Have we made those incredible changes to how we think, or are we really no better than the ant? Yes, we have more energy efficient houses, we put satellites into space, we have wind farms, we have cars that drive themselves we have Wi-Fi, computers and more technology than we know what to do with, but at a conscious level, are we any better off than the ant? As along with all the technology and comforts we have, have we really grown our conscious minds to be better people? Let's face it we still have wars, shootings, muggings, rapes, road rage people getting bent out of shape as someone has something, they don't have etc. I cannot remember the last time I saw on the news that an ant ran a mock in a shopping centre killing people with a knife or gun. Yes, okay it will be a very small knife or gun, but the point is with our conscious minds evolving and getting more complex as it continues to discover, why are we not learning from it. Why then are there situations that we feel we are not in control of from a personal point of view. Our consciousness is why we are evolving, it's a collective process where the thoughts and behaviours of not only us as individuals but of others has an effect on how we evolve. I get that an ant isn't a great example, but the point I am driving is that nature is constant, yet with everything we take away for instance the rain forests the ant is still striving, it, (nature) finds a way around things. This perhaps goes back to chapter two and why we need to adapt and connect to nature more than we do. Collectively we strive to evolve and prosper but yet our consciousness still hangs on to the basics. Why? We have a thinking brain which the ant doesn't have, however, the ant is still here and evolving, where we struggle a lot of the time to make sense of the world around us. Perhaps the ancient shaman, or medicine people were right, in the fact they said that nature will always keep us fed and alive. Maybe not from a sustenance point of view, but perhaps from what she is trying to tell us. As we evolve as a race, we increasingly switch off from nature as we believe we become more powerful and more intelligent to what we think our needs are, instead of listening to the lessons being taught to us. As our consciousness grows, perhaps we need to step back and take note of the past lessons rather than charge head on into the future with no real direction. There are people that have a clear direction and path they have set out for themselves, but collectively as a race of people I am not 100% sold on the idea that we at times move in the right direction. Let's face it, we are destroying the rain forests that are needed to survive and the oceans are littered with our plastic waste that is killing the life within those oceans. Our climate has changed significantly since I was a little boy to a point where weather forecasters get it wrong on a regular basis as patterns constantly change. If we are happy to continue to do that for future generations, then where will this consciousness take us in the future as we continue to strive for the greater good, or are we striving for the good for the greater race on this planet i.e. us? If so, that is a scary thought, as I am not sure where that will leave us all in years to come. I think the time has come, (or is closely coming) that we all need to understand that a collaborative consciousness is needed right across the planet to ensure we keep moving forward in a culture of growth driven by an understanding of the needs of not just us, but of this planet we call home. It's what we teach our children that will ensure we have a good awareness of how collective consciousness plays an important part on how we, as a race, survives and prospers. Let me put this another way culture behaviour is the basics of what every society does under the circumstances it is faced with. Any given social group and the culture it is involved with will be either more advanced or indeed more backward than the other. If the circumstances should change due to population, historical events or environmental change, culture will change and with it our consciousness. And that is what I was meaning by educating our children to realise that as we evolve and those decisions we make, it will have an effect on our culture which will then become our new awareness.

I said earlier that there are two parts the conscious and the subconscious and that the subconscious was more powerful than the conscious. So, what is the subconscious where is it located and how do we know it is there at all. Let's start with the dictionary part which states the subconscious is *Innermost, hidden, dormant, concealed imagination and inner self.* Interesting and yes, I get that, I also got the following from Wikipedia: The word **subconscious** is the part of consciousness that is not currently in focal awareness. The word 'subconscious' represents an anglicised version of the French *subconscient* as coined by the psychologist Pierre Janet (1859–1947), who argued that underneath the layers of critical-thought functions of the conscious mind lay a powerful awareness that he called the subconscious mind. And that I totally get, it's that part of our makeup, that is the more powerful part of us. I also believe as do others that the subconscious part of us is that part we bring with us when born into this world and it is the piece, we also take away with us when we depart from this world. In essence it is us or certainly a part of us that evolves and grows as we do. I also believe it is a part of that quantum soup we looked at earlier and if you are able to tap into the subconscious and trust in it, it will allow you to do greater things in this world than you thought possible. Why? Because it is far more powerful and superior to the conscious mind, that part of us that dies when we do, unlike the subconscious that comes with us. The subconscious acts upon information given to it through the conscious mind as well as our beliefs, thoughts and information we pick up every second of every day. Unlike the conscious mind that switches off or certainly slows when we sleep, the subconscious mind never switches of and is just as active when we sleep as it is when we are awake. The subconscious mind doesn't discriminate, judge, make assumptions or give bad advice. It simply is! But what it does do is help you by giving you those instinct and gut reactions that we need to tap into as we read in an earlier chapter. It is wise and all-encompassing, always guiding us, learning and growing, it is our personal encyclopaedia storing information, ideas theories and giving us the answers that we sometimes struggle to find. It is the source of our creativity and will give us behaviours which are at times not in keeping with the person we think we are. It holds the mystical and the awareness that we are greater than just us. All we have to do is tap into it and trust its directions as it gently steers us through times when we most need guidance. What I find totally amazing is the way it does all that without it really entering our awareness. We are not aware that it is doing this and guiding us which I think proves just how powerful the subconscious is. It isn't a physical part of us to which the conscious mind is, it is difficult to state where it resides. All I can say is that it resides in that part, which is us, the true us, that part, which is not limited by space and time, not limited by the physical or persuaded by outside influences. As a medium and psychic, it helps me to chat or communicate with significant others and for me that's interesting, as when we die and move on do I actually communicate with that person, or is it that subconscious that I am communicating with? I know a lot of you will be sceptical about mediums etc. and that's your choice, but what if mediums are no more than people who are able, for some reason, to tap into the subconscious mind and thus by doing so, allowing it to open and communicate to others around it. Being a psychic, when I am with people, I do this annoying thing of telling them what they are thinking before they really know themselves. Perhaps what I am doing, is communicating with their subconscious and by doing so, allowing their minds to integrate with mine, as let's face it, we are all connected through the quantum soup, so it makes sense that I can connect to them and them to me. One interesting episode around that thought, I was speaking to a friend and sceptic, which, by the way is totally fine with me. When I noticed a shadow around him, it was okay, it was a friendly shadow in the form of a spiritual helper. Anyway, I didn't say anything and up to that point he hadn't seen or noticed anything around him, in fact had never seen anything like that in his life. This shadow came closer and as it did, I turned my gaze to it for a very brief moment. My friend then said, in a somewhat shocked voice, "Oh my gosh," or words to that effect, "What the hell was that?"

I laughed and said, "Don't worry, it is here to help you." He turned quite white as he saw for the first time this shadow that has actually been a part of him for many years.

"Is that what I think it is?" he said in a more controlled voice.

"Yes," I said, "it is a spiritual helper, come to help you for some reason." He then asked me some questions around it and was then more relaxed about the whole thing, if a little wary. Now was the reason that my friend was able to see this being a result of my subconscious connecting with his and as I allow these spiritual people to come close, my friend was also suddenly able to see this helper as our minds were somehow connected? Interesting thought, eh? That on a train I can also do that with a complete stranger, although I don't say anything to them. Perhaps that's the evidence needed to show that we are connected at a higher level, and that higher level is our subconscious minds. The endnote of that, is that my friend is now wanting to learn more about this other world, that some of us call our real home, I will leave you with that thought.

As you can see, the subconscious is far more powerful and encompassing than the conscious part. Both are needed, but, and here is the part that I feel we at times struggle with, both parts need to be in balance with the other in order to get the real benefit and understanding that is required to fully engage in this life. And how would we do that? Firstly, it's understanding and recognising that there are two parts to us, that there is the conscious and subconscious. We can go into the complicated world of theories and ideas thrown up by the various teachings around modern psychology at this point but, as I always like to keep things as simple as possible, I am not going to do that. Just an understating of the basics is all that is needed for you, which will allow an opening of the mind to such ideas. Those basics are, the conscious is engaged in the here and now, it's helping you to decipher the things you hear, see, touch taste and smell. It takes on social conditioning as well as the behaviours of us and those around us. It is a powerful piece of kit and when used correctly it will push you onto many new and exciting journeys while keeping you aligned and open to new ideas and suggestions, if you allow it. Problem is, as well as being powerful it's also a little sensitive. To the point that it allows that thinking brain to sabotage it with what we perceive to be true driven by what we allow people to influence us on. That's where we need that time to stand back look at situations and ideas for ourselves and allow that instinct and good old common sense to intervene and show things for what they truly are. The subconscious, on the other hand, is immensely powerful and always engaging. It is wise, encompassing and resides at that higher level that at the moment is hard to comprehend. It is there for us to use and tap into, again allowing that instinct and common sense to power ourselves across our daily lives. It is engaged 24/7, 365 days of the year and I believe it is more a part of us, if not it is us, that stays with us when we depart this physical time and space we currently live in.

To balance these into our daily lives, we need to understand both components too, which I hopefully have given you an idea into how both interact with us on a daily basis. To bring both into play at any given time we have to do a simple exercise, and that is, for any given situation you need to use **'logic'** *to understand the problem*, **then** *engage* **'instinct'** *to solve it.* There, told you it wasn't complicated. And that's it, that is all you really need to do; if you can practice this again and again so that it becomes second nature, then it will become a part of your daily thought process, which will engage every time you work with an idea, thought, memory etc. What that does is allow you to look at any situation, idea or even a bit of news using the logical understanding that the conscious will engage, if it is encouraged to do so, allowing instinct to bring the answer, idea or thought to you. Not the one conjured up by someone to which gossip intimidation and hysteria are a part of their daily existence. Remember to allow yourself the time to think rationally about that situation. So, stop, relax be quiet and take that daily rush out of your mind for five minutes and allow rational thoughts to come to you about whatever it is you need to think about, and finally, take the emotion out of it. That will allow the quiet logical part of the conscious to come to you. Once you have a quiet true understanding of whatever it is, engage that instinct by trusting those gut reactions and common-sense rationale to flow into your being. Or as you are getting into this routine, meditate for a while on the answer you seek. It doesn't have to be long; a few minutes is all it will take, and the more you practice the easier it will be, you may find you are doing this without even realising. If you do the first conscious part of the exercise and allow logic to enter into your psyche, then you are naturally opening the instinct or subconscious part of your being, you may get the answer you need quicker than you thought. But know what? You will know as your higher self will tell you, through that deep seating feeling of oh yes! That feels so right to me. And allow yourself a smile, knowing at that point you have engaged that all-powerful higher self to come to you, to engage with you and to communicate to you. That my friends is such a powerful thing to do, that once you have experienced it, you will want to experience it time and time again, as not only does it feel pure and magical, it is also the truth and opens your mind to so many possibilities. Go back in time to the greats of Aristotle, Marcus Aurelius, De Vinci, Galileo, Newton and more up to date people like Einstein and Russell all of whom noted the point where they were able to tap into a higher self. Let's face it, they didn't have computers to help them and some of their ideas and theories were so advanced for their generation that they are still in use in our world today. This does work, so trust it. These parts of your psyche, the conscious and subconscious are there to help you so tap into them, understand them, let them into your daily lives. Ignore them if you like it's your choice, but tapping into something that is far more powerful, than you are on this earth at this time, makes sense to me.

Wow! So in this chapter we have hopefully opened your mind to the existence of the conscious and subconscious minds. Both are all-powerful and are required to keep us as humans at a level of continued growth and advancement, however, if they are not understood and indeed misunderstood then they can lead us down the wrong path as we confuse the positive messages they are sending to mean something entirely different. An example of that is the way the conscious mind at times, may give you more questions than answers. That is perfectly fine as it is showing you another way around the problem or issue you are faced with. Don't dismiss it look at it, stand back, be quiet and use logical thinking to understand where you are at that time. Remember the subconscious is all-powerful, there isn't anything higher that you, as an individual, can work with. The conscious is there on a daily basis, to help and guide you through your daily existence. It uses your experiences and develops yours and our culture behaviours using those encounters both personal to you and on a collective level. It is intuitive and develops over time, it is constantly evolving and adapting us to the world around us. Over another 100 or 500 years it will become more advanced than it is to-day as we download more information and upload it to this central data base. When you die so does this conscious mind, unlike the subconscious which never dies and is always a part of you. But, before the conscious mind dies, the subconscious mind, which is hugely more powerful, will take onboard the learnings it needs from this life and updates itself with everything it can learn. Remember the subconscious is capable of taking onboard +17 million bits of information a second. That is incredibly and impressively fast, and you know what? You don't have to plug it in, or update it with the latest software, it does all this on its own and powered by something we cannot comprehend on this earth at this time. The subconscious mind doesn't make assumptions, nor give bad advice, it is that instinct part of us and is forever learning. It is more complicated and powerful than our brains can comprehend. It's connected to that quantum energy soup, part of the invisible and is connected to everything around you. So, why don't we listen to it more, take note of what it's saying and let it guide us? Simply as most of us don't know of its existence. We may have heard of it, but if I asked you before you read this where it is and what does it do, I would say 90% would say that they don't know and that's fine as we weren't really taught about it at school; I was taught logarithms for some reason, but not about why we think and how we think. To use the subconscious, first acknowledge it's there which will be the first step, then remember it will communicate to you through instinct and common sense. Use logic to understand the problem then use instinct to work through it, common sense will follow quickly on. Science is catching up fast, and through modern methods are now understanding about this quantum soup and energy field and realising that the subconscious is a part of this realm. There has to be a balance between the conscious and subconscious minds, using the ideas above will help you understand that balance, but practice tapping into it, understand it and then realise it is there to help you in all you do. It will help shape not only your life but of those around you.

One area we haven't looked at yet, and as this chapter is called the birth of consciousness, perhaps we now need to look at this part now. We have just read about the here and now part of the consciousness and the mystical and deeper subconsciousness. Which brings me to the big question, if the subconscious is actually us, where did it come from and where is it going?

Buckle up this may be a bit of a ride. If we, our spirit, is the subconscious and we are evolving as a race on this planet, where were we before we arrived? I mean look at the dinosaurs that were here 245 to 66 million years ago, which was millions of years before the first homo sapiens arrived. They, I would have imagined had a brain a bit like the humble ant, which is a process driven brain. They died off and eventually we arrived. This is the interesting part, the first homo sapiens must have had a conscious thinking brain as we have evolved from this first basic human type, BUT, did they have a subconscious part to them? I would boldly say they probably did as they learnt, they were expert hunters, learned to survive and build communities, basic ones, but none the less they had them. They had hierarchies and structure and supported each other. They were successful as look at where we are now. Yes, okay, I get it that they were slow starters, however, they did start and they did evolve. To do all they did, they must have developed and evolved the conscious part of the mind, just as we are doing now. Could they have evolved and could they have learned as much, had they not had a subconscious part to their psyche? I would say probably not, as the conscious and subconscious for us as humans come as a pair. Look at it this way, if they just had the conscious mind then who taught them to survive and give them the skills needed? The conscious mind must have been too naive and it was also learning. So, there must have been something higher that was driving and allowing the conscious mind to develop. There must have been a higher force at work, which must have been the subconscious. If that is the case, and this is just a theory, the subconscious couldn't have evolved, it must have always been there as otherwise in the early days, we wouldn't have known what to do, and then later evolve. Wow, what a thought that our higher spiritual selves must have already been in place before we arrived on this earth. If this may be true, where did the subconscious come from? it must have been there when we arrived, to help the thinking mind and conscious part of us to grow. If it was already there, then it didn't evolve, it simply was. and if it simply was, then where did it come from and why didn't it appear much earlier than the dinosaurs, why didn't we come earlier? This throws up all sorts of questions that I am sure one day will be revealed. There are some that say we didn't evolve, we just arrived. Others say God put us here and we just evolved. I get the evolved part as that's exactly what we have been doing over the last few thousand years. But not from the start, what a thought eh? How did we just arrive and have that higher part of us already in place? Did we arrive from another planet? Did God bring our subconscious into life that made us humans the way we are? What happened way back in time to make us different from all the other animals on the planet? Some say we still evolved from a small water-based creature and learned to walk and breathe. Okay then, if that is the case, why do have that thinking part of the psyche/brain that almost no other animal on the planet has? As we read earlier, we are all part of the quantum energy soup, we are all connected to every living thing on the planet. So, kind of interesting that we were chosen to have this thinking brain and not say a Zebra or the Elephant or indeed our humble friend, the ant. Do they have souls and a subconscious? I don't know is the answer, but I would say they must have some kind of variance of it, as otherwise it would throw us off balance, of us all being connected at that deeper level. Another question then, if we all have a type of subconscious that means everything has a higher self not just us, do we all live on after this life? Gosh it must be pretty busy over there. But seriously, I understand the quantum part that says our universe is made up of pure energy and it's how we engage with that energy to determine if we engage with a wave or collapse that wave into a particle. I will add a part here from the encyclopaedia that explains it better:

Wave – particle duality is the concept in quantum mechanics that every particle or quantic entity may be partly described in terms not only of particles, but also of waves. It expresses the inability of the classical concepts 'particle' or 'wave' to fully describe the behaviour of quantum-scale objects.

In other words, it is what we determine something to be that will bring about the change from a wave to a particle. i.e. either a sound wave or a rock. But what interests me is that at the very early start of our being we were already breaking that energy into waves or particles. Therefore, we must have had a higher ability at work that enabled us to do that, as the conscious mind doesn't work from that domain, only on those five senses we still use it for today. So, the subconscious must have already been at work when we arrived to help us navigate the world around us, even though we were basic forms of life. I find this fascinating that at our early times of existence, there was a higher 'self' already at work. Where that came from has many ideas and theories, you will have some of your own no doubt, or even perhaps prefer to be ignorant to it, both of which are fine as it is your life. And to be honest, as it's such a big question, it may be beyond most of us to comprehend. Why? Well, perhaps there are mysteries in our life that are to remain as exactly that, mysteries. If we were to know it all, there may be no point to parts of our lives from an evolution point of view, as we still need to learn and grow.

Before we leave this chapter, I hope this has whetted your appetite in looking for more information on these two powerful parts of us. One more thought, earlier we mentioned that the ant has process behaviour, where it builds its nest in a particular way, which has worked for them for thousands of years and they will continue to form their nest that way as it will struggle to comprehend another way of building it due to its lack of a logical thinking brain. But my thought is, if they have been building it that way for all those years, who was it that told them to build it that way in the first place? Interesting thought?

Actually, as I write this, that wasn't the last thought, as another one has just popped into my mind.

I mentioned earlier that our consciousness as a race will continue to develop and evolve as we grow and learn about ourselves. One thing that worries me, is that as technology becomes our ever-constant companion these days and life becomes faster and more complex. Will we lose that personal growth as we become too reliant on the technology around us? Will we lose that ability to use common sense and instinct, if we can get all we need from tapping a few keys on a keypad? Spiritual growth and indeed conscious growth have to come from within, but will the use of technology stop us from learning from within as everything we need is out there, at a touch of a button, thus stopping us from learning or working things out for us as an individual? Common sense may be a thing of the past as we may become too reliant on phones, tablets, computers and technology to tell us what we need, rather than using common sense and our brains. I hope that as we evolve as a race of people, we collectively remind ourselves that not everything can be learned from technology and that connecting with nature as we covered in chapter two, is just as, if not all important. A civilisation that cannot work things out for itself, by itself by using nature and common sense, instinct and intuition surely cannot survive? Technology can give us a lot, but it cannot give us the will to survive and grow, only we as a collective human race can do that.

Going back to basics will help us remember that we, as a growing race, need the assistance of that ever-present part of nature that is around us and within us. Going back sounds like we should abandon the forward thinking we are presently enjoying. But no, what it does is make us fall back to re-evaluate what's important and help us re-group into that part of our human growth that will allow us the time to see and re-connect to our higher, natural selves. I think if we evolve too quickly and don't allow time for us to fall back, it will be at our future determent. This, I think, leads us into what it means to be human.

Chapter Seven
Human Being

This has the tendency to be a very intense chapter, but as always, I will make it as plain and simple as I can, while opening your ideas to what a human being is. To start as I mentioned earlier in the book, we are spiritual beings having a human experience. That in itself helps me personally understand a little better about who I am. Allow me to explain to help you, understand where I am coming from.

What makes up a human being? Well, there is the physical part, it is what we are physically made of, flesh and bone. We have muscles, a brain, blood running through our veins, nerves, tendons and other material that allows us to move around this planet. I am glad we have all that as otherwise we would be a saggy mess on the floor. The most important of that is the brain, (that as we have already seen, is also part of the conscious) as let's face it we wouldn't get very far without it. It tries to make sense of the physical world, by using our old friends the five senses. Those we use every waking hour which are what we see, hear, touch, taste and smell. We use these to navigate our world and the information gained by these is processed by the different neuron pathways in the brain to come up with tangible ideas and answers as to what we are experiencing on a daily basis. It controls our nerve impulses thus allowing us to move around this world. Everything we witness on this physical plane can be understood in the fact that when we process this information there is a solid foundation behind it. It can be touched, seen, it has a solid base, only because as we touched on earlier, our brains work too slowly to see that things are actually moving in and out of existence. Things in our world then are solid, reliable and two-dimensional. There are laws of nature that guide us through this physical domain for example, the fact that there will always be a cause and effect, which makes our lives somewhat predictable. This predictability allows us to follow patterns in our lives and live our life around a set of processes or principles set down by that mentally restricting 'natural' law of the physical world we live by. We use this physical self to move around our world, it is that tangible part of us that can be observed and understood by others, they can see you and therefore, you are here, a person, a human being living on this planet. There for all to see, the person being observed and the person observing their world i.e. us as an individual human. To sum up the physical part of us, I can say that we see the world and our part in it by the five senses and by our imaginations that uses these laws of the physical to create a world around us that we use to navigate through our existence.

That then takes us to the second part of what makes us human, the spiritual or the subconscious or even the soul, as some people like to call it. It is where I believe that higher part of us lives. We as a human entity, (as covered in chapter six), we need the physical and the brain/mind to move around this planet but without spirit the mind and body are one without reason, they have no direction. The spiritual is that part of us that resides within that quantum soup of pure energy. Without the spirit, the body is like a light bulb without electricity, it's there but there is no illumination. It's not until the bulb has electricity, or in our case the spirit, that the bulb suddenly lights up, or in our case our physical bodies come alive. It is at that point that the physical body becomes intelligent, has an identity and develops a self. This happens at birth when our spirit enters the physical human body. I laugh when a friend of mine says it enters the body at the first time a baby cries, it's almost like our spiritual selves are shouting no, no, I don't want to be a part of this physical world. But enter it does, and in doing so agrees to be that part of us which drives us from that higher plain, if we only take time to listen to it. However, the beauty and grace of the spirit is mostly hidden by the strong self-perception of the body and our material world. We covered most of this in the previous chapter when we read about the conscious and subconscious. So, let's move on as I would like to look a bit deeper, but not too deep, as remember let's keep things simple. Modern thinking about us as humans, is wound around the differences between us and animals what makes us a human vs what makes an animal an animal i.e. what makes a zebra a zebra. I would like to look at this, but also add in some other ideas to make you think. I get it about evolution which we covered earlier in the book and about how we evolved where animals and insects haven't so much as we have a thinking brain and they don't etc. but I feel there is more to be discovered around us as humans that we touched on previously, and as this book is all about getting you to think about things in a different way, then let's see where this may take us.

We, humans, know that we are slightly different to animals due to way we have social, biological and emotional qualities. We are by default social entities and mostly, we look at the world around us and use conscious thinking to build a picture of where we are and what others may think of us and our actions etc. Problem is, as a lot of us are insecure about us personally, a lot of our actions are formed around getting people to notice us, that way we don't have to make the effort to be a little different. Why do I say make the effort? Most perceive that to be you, takes effort, as you may be different to others and that takes energy to be different and not conform to the rest. But you couldn't be more wrong, it takes less energy to be you, just as being happy takes less effort to being sad or upset. Happy is a basic state; it is inbred in us, being sad and angry takes more effort. Let's look at an example: you go to a party have a good time, dance, have a glass of wine and engage with people who are also there to have a nice time. You feel energised, relaxed and you have a nice contented manner. It takes no effort to be in that state, it flows and is natural. Then think about a time when you were angry, fed up, pissed off and really down. Your whole body reacts, your body feels tight, you have headaches, nausea, probably grind your teeth, that fight or flight kicks in and so now you have a lot of excess hormones surging through your body. All that, dear reader, isn't a natural state to be in, as such your body takes a lot of energy to make those changes. When you wake up after the night before, having had a really nice time, you feel good, probably carry on smiling and feeling great. Wake up after a night being angry and upset and you feel like you have a hangover, as all those hormones which have now left your body, leave you feeling tired, lethargic, nauseous and probably in a worse mood than the night before. I know how I would like to feel when I wake up in the morning. Thing is, you don't need to go to that party to make you feel like that, just the natural state of being happy with who you are will bring that natural contented self. Let's look at behaviour then, as being human on this planet will equal the behaviour, we engage within our lives on a day-to-day basis. So, behaviour is 'the way we conduct ourselves towards others' as per the dictionary. I also think it should cover the way we conduct ourselves to us. We are two parts the conscious and subconscious, so perhaps we should be looking at the way we treat ourselves as well as the way we interact with others. It is a part of the human 'being' part that I think is important to cover, as although there is the human vs animal argument there is also the human vs human part, which is unique to us as a human. Look at it another way a zebra is a zebra, it has been for hundreds of years and will continue to be so. It may evolve slightly as its habitat changes, but in essence it is still a zebra. Like the way an ant is an ant and will always be an ant. A human is a human…but wait, hang on here, when we look back over the last thousand or so years, we have changed physically, our bone structure has changed, we walk differently, we think differently, in essence we have evolved and will continue to evolve.

I think in 100 years' time, our thumbs will be double the size they are now as we will need this with all the texting we do on our mobile phones. But seriously, in another 500 years we will have changed slightly from what we are now as we take on new environmental impacts. That's the physical side to us, but what about our spiritual self? Will that continue to evolve? On that, I am not so sure, you see, science is discovering that our spiritual/subconscious selves, due to the fact it lives within this quantum energy soup, where space and time doesn't exist, may in fact not evolve.

As it is already part of the past, future and present, so really in essence we have always had this spiritual side to us, but probably we were not aware of it until the last few thousand years. The point I am making is that if our higher selves have not evolved, (as it is timeless) then it must be our physical selves that change our behaviour as it is present in the here and now. Yes, I know, a long-winded way of saying that it is our conscious ideas, of what we see, hear etc. on a daily basis that runs our behaviour not our subconscious. Interesting thought that if our conscious part of us, which is weaker than the subconscious part is giving us our behaviours, then why are we not allowing the more powerful part of us to help run our lives and our beliefs. So, behaviour is the actions which is measured by ideal standards, those we deem to be acceptable in our society. Which is good as we need a standard common set of principles to live by. The animal kingdom can also be measured in this way, with hierarchy within groups or herds which govern the other members of that group. For us as humans I do feel, and this is just me, but I do feel at times that some of what we think is acceptable is now a little outdated. Yes, we need law and order for the good of the collective, but we also seem to progress further into being a little too clinical in what we feel is acceptable when it comes down to things like humour. I was watching old comedy sketches from the 80s and they had me roaring and laughing, gave me a good feel factor and was a lot of fun and nonsense. Would they be allowed to be shown on primetime TV today in 2018, the answer is probably not, as there are far too many groups who would complain about this and that. But you know, back in the 70s or 80s these comedians were taken at face value and were purely making us laugh with no real malice intended. I still find them funny today, again taking them as a bit of fun with no other intent but to make us smile and laugh. As mentioned, these days everything is far to PC, you cannot make fun of this group or that sect and you simply cannot take the fun out of the gender divide. Just not done these days. I feel that even in this simple example we have become too stiff and what is expected behaviour has changed from plain fun to a 'be careful of what you say, as you do not want to offend'. Just ridiculous. It's fun and it just makes us laugh, but we don't seem to take things at face value anymore, things are getting far too serious.

One example of how I think we have changed over the last 30 years is in places like the office environment, meeting places, restaurants and bars, the street and simply talking to people we have to be so careful we don't offend anymore it is getting out of control. I get law and order, but people we have to let go, relax a little and just take things at face value and not put too much emphasis on all this crazy non-PC environment we are creating. Anyway, of my high horse.

It is interesting though as one of the things that makes us human is our sense of humour. It is our ability to laugh to find things funny and to not take our selves too seriously, which I think is a factor of what makes us human. As although animals have this sense of fun, i.e. throwing a ball for a dog, or watching him/her play with their squeaky toys, you can see they are having fun but I am not sure they would be understanding a funny story. As I have never seen a stand-up comic in a herd of buffalo or zebra. But it is that sense of fun that we have as a trait of human behaviour that I feel makes up that human part of us. As mentioned, the more PC we get about ourselves I feel we may lose that part, which is a shame. Anyway, already covered that off.

That brings me to imagination, which is another human trait that animals don't share and as such it is another thing that makes us who we are. Although these days, I think technology and our society, for what it is, is stopping so many, (and mainly the young), from using their imaginations as it is taken away at such an early age. We have the capacity for great imaginations as it gives us our humanness our creativity, it is, in my opinion, one of the greatest things we can do, but yet majority of us do not use it. In fact, I am not 100% sure how much it is encouraged at school and at play times. I may be wrong but what I see with the children that I have around me, they don't have this abstract thought capability we once had. It's like it has been driven away from them and with it perhaps the ability to use common sense, as we are emerging into a world where we are told more and more what to do and how to think. When I was younger, I used to play in the fields near my house with my brother and sister, we used to ride over there on our horses, tie them up, play for hours, then ride them back home, where we fed and watered them ready for the following day. Did they exist? No, did they have to? No, as my imagination made them real. A close friend of mine has two boys, I was round there on the way home a few weeks ago. The boys had just come home from school and eldest, who is 11, was telling me about a drawing class he had at school. "Great!" I said. "Show me what you can draw," as I was so happy that this young lad was about to use his imagination. I was however shocked when he went to his school bag and produced what looked like an iPad.

"What is that?"

"Oh, it's his work book," his mum stated.

"His what?"

"His work book. All his books are in there and he just selects the class he needs and hey presto, amazing isn't it?" she walked away happily.

I said to Josh (name change), "So, show me your drawing."

He said, "I am, but I need to get the lesson up." He pressed a few apps on this laptop thing and what he learnt that day suddenly came to life in front of us.

I said, "Well, forget that, draw me something, anything!"

He looked at me strangely, then said, "What shall I draw?"

"I don't know something from your imagination."

Then he went to the search engine in this thing and after a while came across a picture, he said, "There, I will draw that."

I said, "No, something from your imagination."

To which his mum said, "Oh, he doesn't need that when everything he needs is on that workbook."

I drove home that night with a numbing feeling in my head, this boy at 11 is being taught NOT to use his imagination. I mean this the way it is intended, what kind of thoughtless children are we brining up if they are not allowed to play and use their imaginations?

Did the great masters, inventors, painters and leaders of the past use a laptop? NO, they were taught to be imaginative, question things, be creative and have common sense. In being so they naturally used that subconscious and tapped into that huge energy soup and instinct to engage their thoughts and ideas. What are we producing for future generations? Yes, whizz kids that can use a computer, tablet, phone etc. But the common sense, instinct and imagination will be a thing of the past. That for me is a scary thought, as then, are we any better off than the majestic animals we see walking our planet that move in a processed behaviour because they don't have an imagination? The answer is probably yes. We will all become a bunch of lemmings following each other, unless you read my first book, (nothing like a little plug). Imaginations are so important, but as we progress as a human entity, are we taking away those important survival instincts? Those parts of us that make us human? Having an imagination gives us the ability to be creative and resourceful, it gives us that sense of wonder and fires the mind into looking deeper into a given subject or thought. Take that ability away from us and we become lost and confused with no direction. Having an imagination opens the mind to possibilities, it allows the mind to flow, be open and be creative. So moving on, I think I have made it clear that we need to teach our children how to play without that technology stimulus we seem to think they need and allow them to make camps in the woods, or make a tent or cave under the kitchen table to hide from the pirates. Sounds childish, doesn't it? But believe me nothing childish about the great inventors and people of the past that were allowed to play and use their imaginations in their childhood and made our lives so much better to-day by realising that the imagination can fuel future ideas and creativity.

The next part to us being human is we are self-aware, not aware which is different. The difference is that being aware is something that we do actually share with animals. We and animals throughout our lives are continually making choices. It has been scientifically proven that animals share a decision process that is similar and closely matches humans. That's interesting as it implies animals are conscious, they have an ability to be aware of their surroundings and thus make choices regarding their environment. But, and here comes the human part, we are not only aware we also have the ability to be self-aware. That is something animals cannot do. You see animals use the conscious and as such are able to make choices, where as we are aware of not only the ability to make choices, but the recognition of the fact we exist, and therefore calculate that choice and ponder the rights and wrongs of making that choice, thus we are self-aware, not just aware. In other words, we have an ability to think of that choice, where as an animal uses that choice without really thinking about the consequences. It doesn't look at what that choice may bring at a later date. Being aware is something we share with nature, but being self-aware is something unique to us humans. This is another trait of why being human is so unique to us, and also makes us responsible and caretakers of the rest of nature that makes up our planet. Being self-aware is the key to our emotional intelligence. Being human means we can monitor our emotions and thoughts from moment to moment which then governs our behaviours as seen previously. What does self-awareness actually give us? Well-being in a state of self-awareness can give you the ability to act from a here-and-now state of mind. It will allow you to be centred rather than being in a reaction state of living. It may give us that outlook of being mindful and not worrying about the 'what' 'the could be' or the 'what if's' That is an important message we may need to understand, as mentioned before this book is to open up your mind and to look at the world around you. Being self-aware is a human trait that makes us unique, it allows us to see where we have come from and where we are going at the same time, if you allow it, it will centre you to the here and now. That again means we can monitor us, as a race and be mindful as to where and what we are doing. Animals don't have that ability, so again they are somewhat dependent on us to ensure we don't ruin the environment for them as well as us. However, we need to be more mindful of this self-awareness gift we have and realise our actions not only have an impact on us, it has an impact on the environment we share with the rest of the inhabitants of our planet. I won't get on my soapbox again, but more and more of being human means that self-awareness is another important unique part of us – being human which gives us an important job to safeguard the planet for all concerned.

Being self-aware, if used properly, can bring us power over our emotions, thoughts and thus our behaviours, it is an important part of us being human and may take away the need to have those reaction driven attitudes. As I just mentioned, reaction that moves us nicely into the next part of us, which is choice, as we take away the reaction part of our psyche, it brings us choice.

So, what is choice? It is the art of choosing between two possibilities, as per the English Oxford Dictionary. Choices fit within a complex probability and within humans is based on conscious decision-making. That in turn gives us that 'free will' behaviour that is not so apparent in animals. We can look at two possibilities and through choices made by analysing these choices we can come up with a tangible answer to go with choice A or with choice B, or in some cases choice C. Having a free will and the choices we make as humans, are bound around things like what life we want to pursue, the interactions we have and what we deem to value in our lives and of those around us. As you can see, these are very much bound around human traits, as animals would not make such assumptions about the worlds they live in, so this is another area that differentiates us and animals. In saying that it would be ignorant not to point out that animals do make basic choices and indeed experiments have been carried out on things like the simple fruit fly, which does by association, make basic choices when going about its short life. But my argument is that we know animals have a limited conscious mind that allows them to interact with their environment. If that environment changes, then they adapt very well and very quickly. That is not driven by choice, more of a deeper knowing, or survival trait that is inherent in most animals and insects that inhabit our world. Do they make that choice or is it the conscious survival process that kicks in? If I give a dog two treats, one tastier than the other and put them side by side which one will be eaten? Answer is both, as they are both treats. But interestingly enough, if we repeat that exercise and this time put a treat and a medication tablet side by side, he/she will eat the treat but probably not the medication tablet. So did the dog make a choice not to eat the tablet because it probably didn't look or smell inviting? The answer has to be yes. Others may say they didn't make a choice, it was made for them at a conscious level as their senses said not to eat the tablet as it didn't smell or look nice. For me, however, the fact remains they made a choice, a basic choice, but they nevertheless made a choice. The difference between us and animals is that we make choices based on what the future outcome maybe, whereas animals make choice but do not compute what the future will bring by making that choice. It's made at that time for that moment and that's it, which when you think about it really isn't a bad way to live. Living in the moment, for now, right here, right now is making a choice for the moment. What may happen as a result of that choice is a future tense, which as humans, we can deal with when that time arises. It's a good way for the psyche to be, you make a choice, it's done, filed away and all good – nothing more to think about. But we don't do that as humans, when a choice comes our way we deliberately think about it, look into the future and wonder what the outcome of that choice will be. We then analyse it some more, then get confused, work out if there are any other options, then worry what will happen if we make the wrong choice, and so the wheel goes round which is being self-aware, (which we covered earlier). When animals make a choice, bang, done, that's it; move on, no worrying about the consequences, as that will be dealt with later. And in fact, often there are no consequences, as life has a habit of helping if you make a choice and put effort in. So, again there are some similar traits between us and animals but it's that human consciousness, that thinking part that separates us.

One other part I want to mention before moving on, is culture. Culture is classed as the customs and behaviour of a group of people or society. It also covers off things like music, art, literature and theatre. This is humanism, or is it? There are those that agree on culture being a process driven behaviour rather than existing in the end result. There has been a culture process that has been shared between certain animals. Although in this, I am not meaning the music, art or literature, as I am yet to see animals settling down in the evening to read a good book whilst listening to their favourite music, well, not yet anyway. So, another look at culture which is the definition that says culture is connected to the behaviour associated to environment behaviour. As culture, behaviour links to the adaption one has to their environment and the societies one finds oneself in. Now, that for me is interesting as animals, or certain groups of animals do by association change their behaviour depending on the environment they are in. This happens during the changing seasons and how that animal adapts to these seasonal changes. Which they do far more efficiently than we do. Also, habitual change and learning can be passed down from one generation to another, so that the next generation adapts differently to the environment than its forefathers did. Why do they need to do that? Simply as we are taking more and more of their land and they have to adapt, they seem to do this as a culturally based change that passes down the generations. So, there are some similarities between certain group of animals and us. What makes the humanism part of culture? There are three main parts to a culture base for us humans and that is involvement, adaptation and consistency. Some argue there are more, but I feel these follow the basis of our human evolution of being part of a processed culture-based environment. Why consistency? Because in our humanness we like to be steadfast and adhere to the same principles and form. We don't like change as that means we have to adapt and that equals having to change our thinking, something we don't like to do. In being consistent it means we like to keep things the way they are, it becomes familiar and unchangeable and we know where we are in the great scheme of things, it drives our behaviour albeit a processed behaviour. Adaptation is being able to adapt to different situations and conditions. Ah! Then we can change? So what I mentioned above about consistency is wrong as I stated we don't like to change. Yes correct, but what I am saying here is that adaptation is a part of culture. However, when we look at our progress as a human race it is that ability to adapt, we are losing, why? Because we have lost that built-in instinct and taught traditions that are fast becoming a thing of the past, those two important elements of us we are losing, which for me are important as without them we start to follow the crowd and forget who we are. We then simply allow ourselves to follow others as we don't have that 'follow your own path' mentality, which equals we simply do what society thinks we should do as we don't have our own minds or ability to think for ourselves. That is very sad but coming true, it is a part of our culture that we are losing fast. How do I know? Because we all start moaning about the same things, we buy the same food we start to manifest into a lemming society living from a set of principles set down by others and we start to follow without questioning. Culture is about learning and sharing meanings and lessons we learn through life, but if we become part of a processed culture then we are already telling our children from a consciousness point of view, that a free mind is not something tolerated in modern societies. Scary thought that we are already taking that ability away from future generations. So culture is not unique to just us as a human as it is also a part of animal behaviour in a lesser extent. The only thing I will say is that in animals it is a learning culture to survive, if things don't change then in humans this could be seen as a negative future if we don't start to use our instincts and question the way things are, we have a thinking brain, we need to learn how to re-use it. To recap, culture is mildly linked to our environment and how we live and adapt to that particular environment and or society. It can be learned and passed down to generations as we change and flow through this and future lives.

There are other parts to us which makes us different to animals, things like spirituality and eroticism which are human traits and not shared with the animal kingdom.

We look to a God to help us move and understand where we are in life, we go to church and worship this God to help with our salvation and to ask for forgiveness and for the love and understanding we look for at times. Eroticism is again something animals don't have; their inbuilt mating process is for survival and re-creating it is not for a social pleasure within pairs or groups. In other words, they mate and that's it, sometimes a few times a year but more often it is once a year during a specific time when the female is ready to 'receive' a male partner. One thing certain animals do share with us, is some have adapted to mate for life just like we do. But again, the mating process for these is again once a year. We as humans have this 'need' at times to mate or make love or have sex on a regular basis. Sometimes this boils down to both or at least one having a sexual fantasy that the other partner will indulge in, and I hope this fantasy is agreed on both sides, but alas, I fear at times this is tolerated on one side only. Anyway, the basis of this is that spirituality and eroticism are also traits of humans which animals do not associate with, which is a result of having that thinking part of the brain. Of course, when you think about it, there are other parts to us that are different to animals, but I believe the above covers the main points as to what makes us human.

Before I finish, there is unfortunately another part to us that makes us human vs our animal friends which is the darker side of human development. We are the most successful species on the planet, we have evolved grown and will continue to do so, we have an immense capacity for good and for knowledge. Why then? Why is it we feel the need to kill and hurt each other? We have killed different species of plants animals and insects at an alarming rate, for what sake? We have everything we need and yet we carry on like we are fearful and insecure, taking because we want, killing for all sorts of reasons, greed, religion, passion, territory, but why? Why would we do that, to the detriment of so many other species that call or called Earth home. We have everything we need, more so than at any other point of this earth's history and yet we take more and more we pollute the oceans take away the rain forests and cause wetlands where there wasn't any, and in fact, drain wetlands where there were some. The wastage of food is just incredible. But why? Is it to create a better world for the masses or for a select few? What makes us human in some ways has a darker side of taking and not giving back. Which animal, insect, plant forest or ocean does that to us? The answer is none, only us. So, having that thinking brain that says we are a better race on this planet than the rest, is quite frankly a disturbing thought if we cannot keep our own house in order. Who in fact, is looking after this planet except a dedicated few that get it? Again, the answer is probably none, so what will happen in 100 or 500 years' time as we continue to destroy our home? We become homeless and then the anarchy will really take a grip, as insecurity builds and builds until it simply breaks and that is a part of being human which to me is unnerving and to which seems to be taking precedence over common sense. We have a collective consciousness that is a part of all of us and that connects us all together. So, if we collectively think that it's okay to kill off other species on this planet, except for a handful of people that are trying to hold back the tide, then it's a sad thought, that we all, from this collective consciousness, say it's okay to destroy life and this planet as it's not my problem. Strange that we can pump money into our future yet are happy for others to carry on destroying the future we put money into. Okay, off my chest, but people, we need to remember that we are a part of nature and she is a part of us, we keep taking away natural resources then we are pulling down our home brick by brick. If we destroy something, we are a part of, it will mean we won't have a home anymore and our supposed need to survival will increase. As a result, our insecurity and fear rises, thus causing us, as a race, to become anxious and afraid. Every insect, animal and plant is there for a reason we take them away then we start to reap the consequences.

One thing I haven't covered is love. We, as humans, have an incredible ability to love and to be loved. Some animals and birds mate for life and will mourn a partner when they depart this world and leave the other behind. If there is one part to us, that is true to us, as a human it is the ability to love and to be loved. There is nothing finer, grander more uplifting, peaceful and yet creative in this world than to love and be loved. But when we look at animals, they are at the most part, happy. The zebra grazing (apart from when a lion wants to eat) they are happy to be next to each other and get on with it. The elephants have an incredible family bond to each other and will help and support each other, as do a pride of lion, the rhino down to the meerkats and animals and birds smaller than that. They are happy they live their lives and to most part are happy doing so. Does an animal have a capability to love? I would say to a point yes, they do. Our dog, Bruno, has a huge capacity to love and no matter what happens to him, when I walk through the door, he is always, ALWAYS there with a friendly excited kiss and always so happy to see me and other members of the family when they get home. We give him love back in how we care for and treat him, that allows him to grow. And I am sure in their own ways animals show that same kind of affection to each other. So, I will say boldly that animals do love and are loved by each other. Is love a human trait? Yes but I shall to go far as to say that this is shared by our friends that live on this earth.

Being human means, we utilise a thinking brain that other creatures that share our planet don't have to the degree that we have. It should allow us to be imaginative and creative, it allows us to stand back and look at the bigger picture. It allows us to work things out and strive to make our lives better, which is all good, but I also think we should keep teaching children to use their imaginations and common sense which will in turn cause the mind to come up with new and innovative ideas. It also allows that person to start looking in a different direction to find the life or path they are looking for. We have the ability to love which I believe speaks for itself, but the basics is that we, as humans, have the ability to love and in return allow love to come to us. It is a basic need, to love and be loved, that's it nothing complicated. Do animals have this ability? I would say that certain animal groups do for sure. I was watching a program on swans the other week. Interesting fact, swans mate for life and it was very sad that during this program one of the swans was killed. Its mate felt the loss of his/her partner and pined itself to death. The Swan rescuers took it to a centre and tried to feed it and bring it back to health but its loss was too great and he/she eventually passed away. Now, what a powerful statement to make at the loss of his/her partner, this swan was so sad that nothing could bring it back from this deep depression. What was that, if it wasn't love? It may be that the swan simply missed its partner and couldn't interact with other swans, however, if that is the case then we would still have a survival process and would still eat and move on. This swan in the program didn't it physically pined as do others, the narrator was stating. Elephants also pine at the loss of one of the herds. A friend of mine lived in Africa for a while and was telling me of a mother elephant who, at the loss of her calf due to illness, carried her calf for miles until they came to a suitable place to leave the lifeless body. What is that if not compassion, and what is compassion if not love? I feel the difference for us as humans is that the need for love and to be loved is instinctive. And yet when that love is not forth coming, we get confused, panic and go looking for it. Unfortunately, we may not find it in the right place as the need for love can take us on a path, we shouldn't be on. It can lead to a confused sense of what love actually is. We find it in all sorts of places, it's not the love we find, it may be companionship, acceptance, respect these are not love states more of a needing state. Problem is we feel that these states give us what we need, however, these states may bring other complications and if not careful, we get into the wrong groups of people which could bring trouble. Then as trouble broods we think this isn't for us, then we go looking for love again and we find companionship etc. and the wheel goes around. That's another difference between animals and us, animals accept love for what it is, we, for some reason think that love is out there to be found. It isn't out there; it is within you. Love yourself first and then you will find that love comes to you in abundance. Think that you need to find love out there, beyond who you are, then that's when the troubles start. Animals simply accept love for what it is, the rest takes care of itself they don't go looking for it. And please do not get confused with mating, which is something completely different to love.

I will leave this being human part at this stage, as I hope that has given you food for thought.

We as humans and our animal friends are different but perhaps not as different as people think. Animals are not 'dumb creatures' they may not have a thinking brain as advanced or complicated as ours, but they do have a capacity to learn and adapt more than we probably give them credit for. Being human means, we can think and we can evolve quicker than any animal in history so far, but it also means we have a responsibility to all the other living creatures to protect and care for this Earth. As we evolve, we will continue to create a seemingly better world for us, but never forget at a subconscious level there is that quantum soup that binds as all together. Therefore, we cannot take anything for granted and as we evolve, we must not forget those that are not evolving as quickly as us and that need a little longer to adapt. Building a future for not only us but for the other inhabitants on this planet is key to not only theirs, but also to our survival.

Chapter Eight
Who Am I?

Why would this question be in a book about being a human whisperer? Why would this question be in any book? It's not a question we ask ourselves very often is it? I wake up in the morning and ask questions like, what shall I have for breakfast? What's on the agenda today? Are the kids up? Are they ready for school? Is there petrol in the car etc. etc. But it's not often we ask, 'Who am I?' We have pondered on it, well some of us perhaps, but again it's not a mainstream question, is it? So, why am I asking it now? On a book that is about us as a human and getting you to ask some of those questions about who we are as a race? Answer that question for me, who are you? I don't care about your name or star sign or where you were born, or where you live, I simply want to know who you are?

Can you tell me that? Truly, tell me the answer to that question? I would imagine you are reading this and saying I know who I am …what? A man, a woman, boy, girl, rich, poor, hungry, full, happy or sad? Okay, this is getting a little heavy so I will explain why I am asking such a question. If I say you are a living being connected to everything and anything being of a universal mind, that was born with no name and will go out of this world with a name someone gave you, so you can have a birth certificate a place of residence and an identity that other people can call you and identify you by. What if when you were born, no-one gave you a name and you went through life without a name? In fact, you had no identity at all, how would you feel? Let me get you to have a look at this in another way, having a name and an identity begins to trap you into being that person, it says who you are, but then very quickly it gives you limitations, it gives you barriers about your life, where you live, who your family is and to a certain point it confines you. People will band you into a place and time that your name and your identity puts you in. You become a prisoner to you, who you think you are as these barriers and identity become the walls that surround you and keep you from seeing the big picture. As talked about earlier, we are a part of each other, nature, the trees, rocks, the guy next door and the lady down the road. But, we give ourselves names and titles to become an individual, so we can make our way in this world. Why? Why does being called, Bob, Tony, Barbara or Anne help us establish ourselves within this world? Is calling ourselves these names causing us to put labels on others as well? Is by doing that also bringing limitations to those people? As we read in my first book, we are constantly putting limitations on what we think we can do by the way we are brought up by well-intentioned family members, or friends, teachers, the media and so on. Having a name can also add to this false belief about who we really are. Let's try an experiment: sit quietly and remove the clutter from your life, by simply focusing on your breathing for a while. Now, once you have calmed your mind, take away your name and your identity. What do you see or feel? How are you reacting through the fact you have taken away from your life as it is now, that part of you, the part that you and others can identify you with? Just sit quietly and let that feeling or thought of not being attached to a name, a person or identity fill your being. How does it feel to you? Each may have a different experience, but I bet most will have a feeling of being empty and perhaps being free. If we take away something that may restrict you, it will allow yourself to see the 'you' the 'I' that is the real you. Take a while to sit and just be, don't attach any label to yourself at this moment, then remind yourself of that name and identity you carry around. Amazing how all the clutter starts to fall back in as you resonate with that person you suddenly become again. A lot of that clutter that lives within your mind is a result of that name and that person the name connects with. Another thought here, just to prove a point and to make you stop and think, we covered this earlier but have a think about this. There you are, reading this book and maybe listening to some music or watching the TV. But who exactly is reading the book, or watching the TV etc.? Is it you, the mind, the conscious person called Bill or Susan? Or is it your higher intelligence that is doing the listening and reading? If it's Bill or Susan, then okay that is you, but I bet there is that subconscious part of you that is actually doing the observation. That part of you that isn't governed by that name we have, if that is so, then it's not you the Bill or Susan it's that higher self, that part that doesn't have a name. If that higher part of you doesn't have a name yet, it's the most powerful part of you without limitations, then it proves that if we go through this life wearing our name like a medal, then the simple act of doing that may be holding you back from the greater part of you. Look at it this way, most everything you do on a day-to-day basis, your behaviour your thinking and your fears, worries etc. are all connected to who you are, which may start with those names, titles and identities we give ourselves. Doing that simple exercise above and allowing yourself to connect with the actual observer, i.e. your subconscious, if done correctly, will make you see that you are capable of anything. But, as our society says, we need names so that we can be identified for all sorts of reasons, then we cannot escape from being called Bill or Susan. The lesson here is not to be trapped by what we tell ourselves we are capable of, just because we attach all sorts of things to that name we are called.

A generalisation here but a true one, if you call a dog a name, let's say, Colin (and why shouldn't a dog be called Colin?), he will associate with that name, he will come when called and be responsive to that name. The interesting point here is that Colin will not become Colin, he will become who he is always meant to be and will always be. His instincts and nature will not change just because we called him a name. He will still carry the same characteristics of that breed, or of his ancestors. He will not show any limitations nor weakness or indeed any different strengths just because he is called Colin. He will respond to that name, because that's how we attract their attention; they know that it is associated to them but it won't change their character, and that's the difference between a dog and us. They use the name as an association, we however, use the name as a badge and it becomes a part of who we are. Nature, animals, birds etc. know who they are, they don't need to associate to a name to become who they are. Let's look at this in another way, when we are born, we are given a name, now there are people that study names, that study is called Anthroponomastics, (gosh, what a name), anyway they study personal names and study the characteristics of those people under that name. What is interesting is that people with the name Bill will follow, albeit it loosely, the traits of all Bills according to onomastics. I get it, but then what about traits from things like star signs and Chinese calendars that put people in the same traits. People are the same no matter if they are Pisces, born on the 14th of April or have the same name as each other. So, why do people show the same characteristics when using an identical name or when under same star sign? I am going to be brave here and have a go at explaining my thoughts and theories. I think it leads to a wanting, to be a part of something that actually means that we are all the same, i.e. we have evolved that we can track most of the same behaviours, thoughts and processes of each other, which means that perhaps we are losing our true identity to the world around us. Maybe we are losing our personalities caused by media and social things like texting etc. Have we lost our way in the pressures of modern-day approach of trying to integrate ourselves with others we interact with? Hence, the reason why we respond to being called Bill, or being a Pieces or being born to the year of the dragon etc, as how can Bill born in the year of a dragon act the same way as a Bill that was born in the year of the goat? To me that doesn't make sense so when considering these archetypes, what actually makes us the same? It could be the fact, we are losing our personalities or our identities due to the modern society where we need to be informed and are losing that ability to think for ourselves. If we think for ourselves, make mistakes and understand what went wrong, or indeed what went right, then we are building personalities. If, however, we rely too much on technology, then we have or are losing that functionality, as we lean too heavily in punching a few keys to give us the answers we seek; and where does that lead? To new generations losing that ability to think for themselves, which may, and I am only stating this, may lead to governments in the future being able to manipulate us more freely as we begin to rely on what we are being told rather than working things out for ourselves, we will lose that common-sense factor that ability to think for ourselves. Scary thought, eh?

This chapter on 'who am I' also brings into play our beliefs, (I covered this in my previous book), however it's always good to go over this important subject and recap on the important parts, as our beliefs will also have an important part to play in knowing who you are. Beliefs are born from information picked up as we grow and then they become part of who we are as these beliefs are imbedded into our psyche. But are they real? They are to us, our individual thoughts on what we can or cannot do. They also cause us to look at what we are as an individual, and these in turn bring about our functionality of what we think is true about us and those around us. What if all those truths we thought about ourselves were wrong? What if 'who I am' was born from false information, just like our names may brand us into thinking because we are called a certain name, we have strengths and limitations. Let me bring in a part from my first book here: 'So are beliefs true? I would be so bold as to say no, a belief is just a thought a memory or even a process we use to make sense of the world around us and to give us what we think we are capable of. It lives in the amygdala part of the brain. *(Now the amygdala is the part of our old survival mechanism which we used during the cavemen times. It basically records anything new in our experience and then compares it against established information already stored. If we have a new experience it will match this new information, if it doesn't recognise the information and records this as new, it will tell us to be very careful and wary.)* The trouble is, if we rely too much on the above and don't break away from the amygdala by recognising those times when it is trying to sabotage us then we become victims of ourselves, and that becomes part of who we are, what 'I' that may give us limitations. So, in looking at who I am we also need to understand the sabotage process that will take us away from what we are capable of toward what we think we are capable of, to having strong beliefs about yourself is a good thing, as long as these beliefs carry the following. Firstly, you are happy with who you are, that you have that deeper knowing of that you are actually capable of anything you put your mind to. Secondly, step out of your comfort zone at least once a day. It doesn't have to be a dramatic step just one that will allow you to experience something new. This could be as simple as going to a different supermarket to shop, or taking a different route to work etc. It is a simple act of trying something new and embracing it. Thirdly, live in the moment, remember the past is just a memory, the future just a thought, but now is where the living happens. Now is happening, it isn't in the past yet nor in the future, it simply is. Each day just live in the now as I promise you, if you practice this and you bring it into your existence, wonderful things start to happen. You start to become calmer, you think with a clear head and mind, and you bring the help of that higher power to guide you. Trouble is we always live from those if's and buts and those 'I wonder what will happen if I…' we then get in our own way and stop all the good from helping us. Living in the now, is one of the most powerful experiences I have known it really does work. And fourth, is simply to love. Love yourself, those around you and allow yourself to be loved, not just us humans but nature and all she brings you. When I say love yourself I mean love 'you', the person you are, warts and all. You see if you don't respect yourself and have pride and love in all you do, then how can you love others? I mean truly love others. If you bring love to all you do, then you are tapping into your higher self and allowing all that wonderful energy to come to you. It also brings an understanding, calm, a sense of being and also opens your mind to those all-important possibilities that you may be capable of anything. I would welcome that into my life every second of every day. Is that being soppy? No, is it being realistic and allowing you to grow? Yes. It doesn't take much just a little bit of effort to bring that awareness to help you find that 'I' that recognition of being you. We have seen the I, but who is the who? No, I don't mean the 70s pop group, I mean the who, in the 'who am I?' If the 'I' is the part of recognising you and the awareness of what that recognising brings, which is that love you bring yourself and others, if you only believe in yourself and your capabilities, by letting go off the everyday confusion. But where does the 'who' come into it? The who is simply you, that person that resides in that human body, that observer of everyday life that makes assumptions, makes plans and takes on seven million bits of information every second to make sense of the world around them. But that 'who' is also the unseen part of you, that subconscious we mentioned and covered earlier. It's that part that is more powerful than the everyday you. That's an interesting quote, that 'every day you'. Interesting as that actually says that the everyday you, may switch off every night, in fact it does, it allows your conscious mind to sleep and switch off. However, the subconscious part of you never sleeps and is active 24/7, 365 days of the year until you die, and then guess what? Yes, it goes with you, so it NEVER switches off at all, never. That's a deep and meaningful thought and one which I am sure we will cover one day, when science makes those breakthroughs, if in fact they ever do, as I am sure there are secrets we are not allowed to know. The conscious then is part of our everyday selves where the subconscious is our true self. So, when we couple both together it now looks like: Who Am I? **Well, it's the subconscious real self that when consciously allowed, brings with it the love, understanding and awareness of who you really are. You as an individual and you being connected to everything on this planet, we live on.** Why don't we see or feel this every day? Because we allow that every day to cloud our minds our judgement about the world around us as perceived by others and then passed down to you through the news, TV, media and other mediums of information that paints a very unreal picture of who we/you actually are. Become that 'I', become that person you are, let go of fears, worries and false hopes, just allow yourself to be still every day and be in the moment. Forget yesterday and tomorrow and simply stay in that moment with a clear and open mind and allow your true self to come through and then trust what it is telling you. If you can change your mind about you, then you are making choices; if you create choices, you begin to look at possibilities and ask questions. If you ask questions, then you begin to change the perception of 'who am I', which is one of the biggest questions you can ask. If you can practice that on a day-to-day basis, then you will start to open a dialogue and you will begin to really know who you are. One of the things you are is a miracle, why? Because in your beginning, there were 300 million sperm that started a journey, but only three million found their way into the uterus, that's only 1% chance of that egg being fertilised. The odds on you making it further than an egg are massively against you, but here you are breathing the air on this world of ours, so that in itself says you are a miracle to be here at all. Who you are is a wonderful creation and you are privileged to be here, so don't waste time on the things that don't belong to you i.e. the wrongful reporting and self-sabotage caused by the incorrect information passed onto to you through the fearful masses. Take control and be the person you are. Start to look and challenge your mind-set about who you are, listen and then ask more questions, this process will really open your being to that 'I' that 'who' of you. Let's take a moment to look at this in another dimension, if I say to you, you are what you think, you may say yes I am a man, a woman I am busy I am tired and so on. But I want to explain something to you here that will give you food for thought about the person you are. In the brain is a small part called the hypothalamus, the hypothalamus is that part of the brain responsible for producing hormones and regulating body temperature. It's the hormone part that I am interested in. The hypothalamus basically produces chemicals in response to our emotions. These chemicals are called peptides. They produce peptides in response to anger, sadness, lust, tiredness etc. As soon as we feel that state in our minds or a response from our bodies, the hypothalamus will go to work in assembling the peptides needed to match that emotion and then release these peptides into our blood stream. What happens then is these peptides will go and look for the cells in our bodies, to which we have 37 trillion. Our cells have receptors on them which the peptide will attach itself to, this then sends a signal to the cell with that emotion the peptide is representing, the cell will respond accordingly by changing its state. The cell is the smallest unit of consciousness within our bodies if that changes then we do. As a result, you can see that we are a result of what we think. We have those emotional thoughts and the hypothalamus simply obliges, the body adjusts and we become that emotional state. Problem is, we become more of what we think we are and we start to look for more of it as we are becoming that emotion. If you cannot control your emotional state, then you become addicted to it as it becomes you. Years of emotional abuse will age us and make us prone to disease due to the mitosis division, where the cells in our bodies divide, they will start to build more emotional receptors and less receptions for important chemicals like proteins, needed to keep our minds and bodies in good condition. It is important through our physical, emotional and spiritual selves to keep that balance, sure we will have emotions, it is a part of who we are. But don't become that emotion, understand it, know why it is there at that moment, what's driving it, then as a result fix it, if it needs fixing. If it's anger, hate, sadness, know what's causing them then let it go. On the other hand, if it's love and happiness, then keep it. As covered in my first book, I know that being on this planet is a learning curve, there is dark and light, hot and cold, however, we need to keep that balance. So, bathe more in the sun than in the shadows, laugh more cry less and above all love unconditionally and allow yourself to be loved. To try and make you understand a little more, most of us, due to having a detachment from our emotions i.e. we just let them happen without really understanding why, we will start to live from the experiences of the past, as the conscious mind builds up a picture of what it needs to keep us safe from physical and mental issues. As such we are not operating from a whole, as although we live now, a part of us is always living from the past due to our conscious minds using past experiences to guide us at this moment, which goes back to our beliefs of who we are that we covered earlier in this chapter. I hope by understanding the physical way our bodies react to our mental emotions it will make you realise that you are more in control of you than you think.

In this chapter, I wanted to make you have a think outside of yourself and make you stop and ponder who you are. As I always say, this is personal to each and every one of us, so take time to see you and don't judge yourself against the next person, we are taking about you here, not your neighbour. The next chapter we are going to explore more about beliefs and what you are capable of now you understand more about 'Who am I'.

Chapter Nine
What Am I Capable of?

What am I capable of? Good question and a big question, for this chapter we are going to tackle this in two parts the physical and the spiritual. Like it or not, or believe it or not, we are two parts that I hope you reading this book thus far has shown to you. Let's look at the evidence, you are of two parts the conscious and subconscious, you know that the conscious guides us through our daily lives and endeavours to make sense of the five senses we navigate our world by, in essence what we hear, see, touch, taste and smell. The subconscious is much, in fact, hugely more powerful and is that part of us that is higher than our physical selves and the senses we use to navigate our physical world. For this chapter I am going to use some of my first book, to be honest, I think it covers this part well and as it is already written then why not. Despite what you have been told as you have grown and made your way through this life, you are capable of anything you put your mind to. I understand that sometimes a physical disability will hold you back, but in general you can do anything you want to do. Some people will say oh yes easy to say, but I don't have the money, the time, the energy, the standing to do all I want. That my dear reader is just a state of mind about your beliefs about what you THINK you can or cannot do. That old saying that 'if I think I can or if I think I cannot', you will be right in both cases'. Why? Because it's that story, we tell ourselves of what we think we are capable of. If I say I would like to run a marathon next year, I will start the training, maybe start with some coaching from either a professional, or someone that has already run a marathon. (There are a lot of people out there that can help and at a minimum cost, it just takes some time and energy to find them). Then start your training slowly and build up to it, take the right nutrients, eat the right food and more importantly, have fun doing it. Then, hey presto, a year later you are ready. You may not be the fastest to run it, but if you have had fun, do the right kind of training then there is no reason you cannot compete. Anyway, who said you have to be the fastest, this is your personal journey and your personal achievement we are talking about here. It's the same for anything you want to achieve. You just need to take time to look, understand what's involved and then with a little bit of effort and dedication you will achieve it. As we saw in the previous chapter 'who am I', it is the realisation that taking away that everyday clutter and the switching off to people telling you this and that about what you can and cannot achieve. And by simply loving yourself for who you are and allowing that higher subconscious to come to you by being still, will alone start the process of you being able to achieve anything you want. Accept people will want to achieve different things, which is totally fine, it makes the world go around. Stop looking at what that person next to you is doing, they are doing what they want to do, follow your own path and become the person you want to be. Be you and as long as it doesn't hurt anyone else in the process and you understand the rules then follow your path. People who follow others are just doing what others do, and by doing what others do, we start that process of becoming a collective race of people, or lemmings. What works for one person may not work for others and that's okay, it's called self-discovery. Work out what is best for you, and if you are afraid of scorn from others, well that's only because others may be jealous that they are not doing what you are achieving. Sometimes, when doing new things or trying new ideas we come across a tiger, a tiger, you shout! Yes, a tiger. Let me explain. I once had a very interesting conversation with a Chinese Buddhist monk, wonderful man, full of sense and calm. I asked him that in life we have challenges and that sometimes I find it difficult to find a way around these situations. He said, "Why are you trying to find a way around them? You should embrace them." I said why should I embrace challenges; life is hard enough.

"Because without challenges," he said, "you cannot have growth, you cannot truly be the person you are meant to be." And as I like to put something tangible to explain things, I call life challenges 'a tiger on my path' i.e. something I wasn't expecting to find on my journey. But something I can work through, understand, grow from and walk on. As my monk friend states, we only get these challenges when the universe knows we are ready to deal with it, whatever it is, and the point is to understand what the challenge is and why it arrived at that particular time of our lives. So, let's look closer at our belief pattern, as I would rather understand something than to run away from it.

You see it is nothing but our beliefs about what we are capable of which comes from times we tried something or indeed thought about doing something. Then that old self sabotage kicks in and says no! I haven't got what it takes to do that or try that particular thing. Our minds are always trying to keep us away from danger and harm, by reminding us of times when things we tried, saw or heard what went wrong, or indeed things that caused us to feel fearful. It's those times when the flight or fight response kicks in, that self-survival mode that makes us either run away from the danger or fight it. However, I have a theory, because of our inquisitive minds, if we are not aware of why we need to fight or run, we sometimes analyse too much on that situation or issue. I am sure sometimes you catch yourself asking why am I scared of spiders, or what went wrong the last time I played golf, or why I cannot run, or study etc.? So what happens when you ask yourself these questions? Well, I think you probably say, well it's just who I am. But how many of us have asked ourselves the following question, **but what if I am wrong?** What if that belief I have is born out of false information I received? What if everything I were told about that particular negative belief I have about myself is wrong and has always been wrong? What happens then is you open that dialogue of challenging that part of you, that negative belief. If you change your mind about you, then you are making choices, if you create choices then you look at possibilities, which in turn begins that question process, that leads to changing the perception of what you think you can or cannot do. Remember here, if you think you can or if you think you cannot then you will be correct, but what we want you to do is start that **Yes, I Can** mind-set. By realising that what you believe about you, will start to manifest in your life, so, get that 'believe I' can mentality and use it always. Take the time to identify that part which is sabotaging you, look at it for what it is which in most part is nothing more than a thought planted there by yourself or by someone else you have spoken to, or perhaps you read somewhere. Question that part and then make a choice to move past it, or let it continue to run your life, after all it's your choice.

Let's look at this in another way, the majority of our beliefs are outside of our conscious awareness and do not come into play every second of every day. Only when that memory is fired by a situation or thought we have limiting self-beliefs on, or indeed a similar experience that the conscious has made a close match too. One way I find of getting over these kind of uneasy feelings, or fear, nerves etc., is to remind yourself, that the event or issues you are facing, is in fact a new one and hasn't happened before in your life and in fact may never happen in that way again. It doesn't matter if you have faced a similar experience in the past, this is a new one, and no two events are the same. For an example, you may drive the exact same route to work every day, but every day that route will be different. You may see different cars, the weather will be different, you may see different people, see things you didn't notice before. In fact, the list will be endless, so, when thinking about an old experience from the past that you may be facing again now, just say to yourself:

'I know this is my consciousness protecting me, but this new experience hasn't happened before nor will it ever happen again. So, in effect these feelings are not real, as this experience has not happened therefore, I cannot

use the old feelings, so I will just go with the new experience and enjoy the journey.'

Understanding the above, will make you realise that you are more in control than you thought. Your mind has to work for you, you cannot be a slave to that conscious behaviour which was driven from a past experience or by a well-intentioned someone, telling you what you may or may not be able to achieve. Most of the time it is that model of behaviour that was planted years ago. You can change it, as beliefs are the one fundamental part of our thinking which can hold us back, or indeed push us forward to new heights of achievements in all parts of our lives. What I would like to do now is stop looking at what is holding us back and now start to get you looking at things in a different way and manner that will enhance your lives and help you move forward. Remember life is an illusion, our fears, worries, unhappiness as well as our achievements, successes and happiness all start with what we think we are capable of, and that all starts with what we believe.

How do we change a negative thought about ourselves into a positive one? Well, if you get a copy of my first book *Get Out of Your Way* it will explain this in greater detail. At this point, I just want you to realise that if you can understand why something is holding you back you can change it very quickly by challenging that old thought you had about that particular issue. This will also involve a little bit of energy and effort, remembering not to listen to others, and understand a challenge is just that, a wonderful way in which you can get to know yourself better and grow within this life.

I hope that helps you to comprehend what may be holding us back from being able to achieve and understand we are capable of anything as long as we just take the initial time to realise us/you and the challenges being presented. So, now to that spiritual side of us, that unseen part, as to understand both parts will bring about a whole person we want to achieve in your mind and thoughts.

What is the spiritual? Am I going to become all mystical and start wailing? No, but if you would like to do so it's not a problem. Seriously, I have been a medium and psychic for many, many years.

It started when I was 10 years old, which is the first time I felt a little different to others; I say 10, but I may have been active long before then and just not realised it. I am still me, and as in my later years when Christine, a friend and mentor who has honed by gift, I realise that I will always be me. Being a medium and psychic for me is a natural thing, as science is now discovering. I don't do rituals or dance around stones naked, (although I must try that sometime), I am the same old inquisitive, pub visiting food loving me. What this 'gift' does do for me is allow me to experience life from another perspective and engage in nature, as we read earlier in the book. It opens my mind to possibilities that I was asking when I was a young lad at school, which quantum mechanics is also just discovering. We covered in the previous chapters that we are all connected from a quantum energy soup that binds us all together that ebbs and flows through all of us to all of us. Not just us humans but to everything else you see around you, the trees, grass, birds, animals and even the clouds that pass us by. It's that gap and space between us and fills the skies. It is us, and I believe that our subconscious is a part of this energy and that this part of us goes with us when we pass. Just my theory, but as we recently found out with the discovery of the long-anticipated Higgs Boson particle and other experiments, science is discovering that matter, can possibly travel up and down throughout periods of time.

That is where my theory comes into play, that as our subconscious is made from a higher source yet to be discovered, that when we pass, we are able to move up and down timelines. As that is a big ask for you to get your heads around, let's park that idea for now, but if energy can communicate then being a medium is simply a way that I and others can communicate to those that have passed by simply connecting with their energy. Is it a gift? Yes, but then others on this planet have other gifts in other ways. It's just a part of life that

I have grown up with and that I can use, just like others can do things like play the piano, others are masters at mathematics and some can drive a formula one car at breakneck speeds around a circuit. We all have our gifts, we just need to realise what they are. Enough of this rambling but it is important to realise that being able to speak to people that have passed away, may be just the case of being able to tap into their energy field. I think at times, some people like to inject the theatrical into being able to speak to others that have passed, which may scare some people away, and of course our friends the movie makes love to exploit this area. Believe me, majority of mediums are very normal and last thing we want to do is scare anyone.

As I think the subconscious is us, I mean the true part of us, let me explain why this is important in this part of what we are capable of. The spirit part of us or the spirituality part of us is so important. Spirituality is not about religion, it's not even a cult or a hippy movement, but it is the essence of who you are, why? Because it is part of that subconscious part of you. That part of you that processes in excess of 17+ million bits of information every second. That is why I say it's so much more than religion, or a cult etc. as that uses rationalism to make sense of the world, where your subconscious is the world. When you chose to come back to this earth plane, (and yes you did make that choice, you even chose your parents and the circumstances). Why? Because part of being on this planet right here right now is to learn, this is a huge classroom, where we pick up ideas, theories, we work our way through life and when we pass, we take that learning with us and we have a debrief about what we learned, so we can pass that wisdom onto others to basically help them and in doing so, it helps us to grow. If that is the case, and I have a lot of evidence to point out that it may be, then how do we become more spiritually aware. I have found that I naturally become more spiritual when I stop thinking that I am two-dimensional and believe that I am a part of something much bigger. It takes time and practice to believe that, as modern life, although open to more ideas than in the past, still thinks that this is it and that projects onto our everyday lives. We think that we are born, grow up, work, play, get a mortgage, have a family, retire and die, and that's it. For some there is no other way of looking at life. I sometimes take the train to work and watch all my fellow commuters doing what they do on a daily basis. And yes, we have to work, to get money to pay for things but when I watch the faces there isn't any real injection of life, they are just doing the same as the majority of others. They may get some satisfaction of doing a job well done but for me watching these people, there is no real excitement or wonder about life. We are that two-dimensional being we are taught we are through modern life and its modern philosophies and media stories. Where is that three-dimensional realisation of being a part of something much, much bigger? When we look back through history, the ancients understood more about life than we do now. The indigenous people of North America, those I have a fond connection with, the Mayans the Sumerians, Ancient Egyptians the Kazakh of Asia and closer to home with the Druids. They all knew and understood the spiritual side of life and worked with nature to bring what they needed. However, with modern thinking and technology we are moving further away from these ideas and learnings, which is a shame, as when you look back these ancient people they were capable of a lot more than we are today. Their structures and buildings were built without computers, just their understanding and of working together using a collective imagination and being able to work around obstacles in their endeavours to forge ahead with their lives. If these people who we class as 'uneducated' were capable of this, then why cannot we as educated people do these things? If you just open your mind to the fact that we are three dimensional, as we have explored in the previous chapters then all life becomes open to you, there isn't a time when you will feel alone or two dimensional as suddenly nature starts to reveal herself to you. Being open to things around you gives you that three-dimensional image of your world, it allows you to see and sense things you haven't noticed before. It also becomes your world, as you start to become more in tune with it. And if you start to become more in tune with it, then you realise you are capable of anything you put your mind to. Remember, this isn't a religion or a cult this is just a way of being or connecting to the world around you. First you have to get into your head that you are a part of something bigger. You are connected through, the yet invisible, energy soup that combines us all together and forms our world. That in itself is the biggest part to get your thinking around. Physics is almost there, as they are discovering that we are all part of this quantum soup of energy that binds us all together, every living thing on the planet is bound by this invisible energy. We can feel it, or at least you will once you start to open to this idea. I, and others who have migrated to this higher sense, feel it every day and when I take five minutes to become quiet, I can sense this energy field within me. You can too, because if you can feel this energy that drives and is a part of your subconscious then you can really become and do anything you put your mind to.

How does the spiritual drive the physical? I will take a further paragraph from my first book. Our sensory idea about everything around us is simply created in the imagination. Take the wind, for example. We cannot see the wind, but we can see the effects the wind has on the trees or on our face and bodies. You can see the movement something has on another thing, even if you cannot see it. But, you trust it's there because of the effect it has and the fact you can see the evidence, i.e. the trees moving in the wind. What I am asking you to do here is trust that the spiritual has an effect on the physical, even if you cannot see it, the spiritual will move you and make your physical world come alive. It does this 24/7 every second of the day the week and year using this invisible energy that brings the imaginable into existence, by bringing this invisible energy that is created in your subconscious mind and making it tangible from a sea of endless possibilities. This energy is not of this physical world but comes from a place where your subconscious is also found. Another way to look at this is be aware of everything you see from a physical point of view using your senses, what we see, hear, touch taste and smell, then think who is creating what you choose to see or hear.

There is a larger part of you, the unseen that is working behind the scenes invisibly creating and decoding what you are physically noticing and making sense of. The physical then is the atoms and molecules of the world round you. The spiritual is that higher subconscious part working behind the scenes, creating what it is you are experiencing in your life. Put this into context, if you choose to do something with your life, recognise that it is the physical part of you doing that thing. Now realise that there is a higher part at work brining that experience to you. So, choose to do that thing in life but then allow the subconscious that higher spiritual part of you, to help you achieve it. Remember if you choose to do something, or not, then you will be right, as it's your choice to do that thing, or indeed not. I will ask you a question! Are you capable of doing that thing you want to do? If you understand the above, then you will know the answer, if you still say no, then what is stopping you from tapping into the higher self? To realise that with imagination and a bit of planning you can achieve anything. Need more evidence? Okay, let's try this; I want you to close your eyes, yes okay you need to read this part first then try it. So, close your eyes, I want you to imagine a nice juicy, yellow lemon. It's soft to the touch and you can smell its citric goodness. Now, I want you to cut into it, see the juice running down your fingers, now lift a slice and put it in your mouth. Sense the juice dripping onto your tongue, what happens? Is your mouth salivating? Yes? Then good. But, hang on here, that didn't physically happen. It was a perception and idea of what is happening due to your brain not being able to work out what is real and what is imaginary. You see, your brain doesn't work in logic, only in what is plausible, give your brain/mind something that it thinks is happening and it will react accordingly, as it won't know either way. It will not be able to ascertain if what is happening is real or not but you do. You know if you are tricking your mind or not, so who is actually doing the tricking? It's not your physical mind as you know that you are tricking it, so there must be another part of you other than your physical mind that is doing the tricking. Interesting, isn't it? That at that point two parts of you are at play, the part that is being tricked and the part that is doing the tricking. Are you getting the point now, that there is two parts of you, the conscious and the subconscious? Use the conscious to make the decision to do whatever it is you want to do. Then use the subconscious into tricking the conscious that what you want to do is already happening and then the conscious will respond by making the physical body act in that way. It will take practice but try it, make it fun, but more importantly, realise that when doing this experiment there are two parts at play that you may not have understood before. Remember, we are a spiritual being having a human experience.

To recap, the physical side to what you are capable of starts with the understanding of who you are, that really you are a miracle to be here at all. Don't take second best, be the person you are.

Then comes the physical part that states that, if you take time to realise that blockage, that 'tiger' moment is a challenge that you need to overcome and by taking the time to remember that anything is possible if you understand the challenge. This challenge may be something life has thrown up, or in fact something you want to achieve. Beliefs are just that, it's something you think is true to you, due to circumstances in the past that has stopped you from achieving that goal, or simply something you have been told or read. Beliefs are just part of the story of who you think you are vs who you actually are. Remember 'if you think you can or if you think you cannot' it will be true to you. Before we move on, I would like to bring in something about beliefs that I also covered in my first book. There are lots of stories and some new ones on where humans have achieved great feats of strength and power when it is needed. A lady in America picked up the car when she mistakenly ran over her baby while reversing from the garage. A friend rushed over to help when this 5-ft 4-inch lady picked up the side of the car so that her friend could retrieve the baby from under the wheels. The police couldn't believe she did it, she tried to show them again but of course she couldn't. Closer to home, my sister who is 5 ft with a disfigured arm picked up my dad and rushed him indoors after he hurt himself fixing a car. Again, after the event, could she do it again? No, no way she could pick him up. What happens at these times? Do we say oops! Something has happened I better spring into action. That car looks heavy, or gosh not sure I can pick up my dad. The answer is no, something has happened and I need to fix it. Does the belief come into action? No, you just do it, at that time, at that moment you don't have doubts you just do what needs to be done. You weren't limited by your beliefs and thoughts about possibilities you just did it. So therefore, you didn't have any limiting thoughts about what you were capable of, your body just carried out your instructions at that time. Amazing isn't it? That if you went through life like this with no 'misconceptions about what you could or couldn't do, imagine what you could achieve, in fact, your life would only be limited by your imagination or lack of it. Food for thought, but if you want to believe, you can change that mind-set, ask questions and change that belief. If you change your mind, then you change your choices. If you change your choices, you will begin to look at possibilities and ask questions. If you ask those questions, then you change your perception about who you are. Then there is the spiritual, this higher self that is more powerful than your conscious self. You can start to tap into that by simply realising that there is two parts to you as a human being on this planet. The physical you and the spiritual you.

To start to bring the spiritual into play, first recognise that there is the subconscious/spiritual self then take a little time to integrate it into your daily self. Just because you cannot see it, it doesn't mean it doesn't exist, as you can see the effects of it in your daily lives. Remember the experiment with the lemon, you tricked your mind into believing something was true and happening, but who was actually doing the tricking. Your subconscious picks up 17+ million bits of information a second and never switches off. So, take time to be quiet and tune into it by letting every day clutter go as most of this noise is driven by people and experiences outside of your control. Instead let this inner strength come into your being and feel its powerful, calm and common-sense self. For so long you have probably bought into the idea that we have no control over our lives that we are conditioned to think and believe we cannot make changes, which couldn't be further from the truth, we have choices and we can make changes. As you begin to realise this spiritual self exists, your perceptions may change as well as your environment and how you see yourself within this environment. Change is the only constant within the universe, go with it, but more importantly understand it, it's not a hippy cult thing, it is who you/we really are. Science is really beginning to get a grip of this and understand that we are made of a much higher source than once thought. And I think deep down, we already understand and know this. It's just been hidden within our modern world with its technology and some false beliefs and controlling ideas by the media and some well-intentioned teachings that may be a little out of kilter. Start to meditate when you can, tune into that inner you, meditation doesn't have to be a half hour session, you can start by gently practicing your breathing and taking just five minutes to be still. Below is a simple breathing exercise that will help centre you and start to tap into that inner you.

First just allow yourself to breathe, so take a nice deep breath in through the nose, hold for four seconds then exhale deeply through the mouth. Do this three times, then breathe normally.

Now I want you to fully be aware and concentrate on your breathing. The way I found works is by counting on the inward and outward breaths. Count for four seconds while you breathe into your nose, then hold for four seconds, then breathe out through your mouth slowly for six seconds, hold for two seconds then repeat the process. Keep doing this for as long as you can, to start with try for five minutes then build up to 10 and then 15 minutes. Just allow yourself that sense of calm and peace to enter your mind and body. Your mind will initially try to bombard you with thoughts, things you should be doing in fact all manner of things. Why? Because that's what we do, we are thinking machines. During this mediation have the luxury of not thinking about anything, just be. When you find your mind starting to wander from the counting and concentrating on your breath, just gently bring your mind back to the exercise. Don't get cross or frustrated. This letting go takes some practice, but the more you do this the easier it becomes, so stick with it. Once you become comfortable with this, you will be able to determine the thoughts that are just clutter and those of a deeper meaning, which you need to take note of. Just for now, practice this breathing exercise and allow yourself that wonderful luxury of just switching off.

Try and do that when you can and see if you can make it a daily treat. Why a treat? Because if you can switch off from the everyday clutter you are freeing yourself from daily troubles and strife and simply allowing your mind some 'me' time. Try it! You could be amazed at how calm and fresh your mind feels afterwards. As I mentioned above, practice this and you will see what thoughts are: just everyday clutter and noise. Then once you can do that you are beginning to tune into that subconscious that will bring you a deeper understanding of you and of those around you.

Another area that can help is mindfulness, this is the act of just allowing yourself to be and live in the now. There are a lot of teachings etc. but when you ask a master of Zen, they will say that being mindful is living for now within this space and time. How do we do this mindfulness? The first thing you can do is to start getting into the mind-set of living in the now, simply put 100% focus on the thing you are doing. For instance, if you are having a shower then concentrate on the shower and nothing else. If you are cooking a meal, then concentrate on the meal and nothing else. If you are making a cup of coffee, then again put 100% focus on making the coffee. Doing this will also concentrate the mind on the present here and now. It allows the mind to not only concentrate on the task at hand but it also allows that higher energy to come to you. Don't multi-task, do one thing at a time and take your time doing it. Yes, I know in our fast pace lives we sometimes have to do two things at once, but does that achieve more? Probably not as you are giving two tasks 50% of your effort. Try picking the most important at that time and do that 100%. You may find you are more efficient at doing that one task which will then leave you time to do the second one. It's not a race, before I started this process a few years ago it seemed like the day was a manic place from rushing from one thing or meeting to the next. Was I more effective? No. Did I do more work? No. And did it bring the desired result? No. Because I was busy rushing around, I didn't know what the desired result was. Now I plan, I see, or feel the result I need. Then I go at a steady pace to which I take my time, focus on what I am doing at that time and the rest takes care of itself. You know what? It works and I get the result, sometimes not in the way I envisaged, but I still get that result. At the end of the day I am more relaxed and energised to carry my day into the evening with my family. This doesn't only happen at work obviously, I do this to any task or sport I take part in. I see or feel the end result whatever it is, then I forget it and go at my own pace allowing the help offered to come to me. The last part is an extract from my first book but doing daily meditation and being mindful in your day minute by minute can bring you to a place of calm where the higher self resides.

I hope this chapter has allowed you some airtime to understand what 'I am capable of', which is just a case of balancing the physical with the spiritual. Use the conscious to understand something in your life, then allow the subconscious to bring the solutions, as let's face it you are capable of anything you put your mind to, or not. You can believe in the spiritual, or not. You can believe aliens exist, or not. It's only your perception of what you are allowing your beliefs to tell you. Interesting thought, isn't it?

Chapter Ten
Learn

In any part of being a whisper of our world is that ability to learn and extract information from our lives so that we can use it to better ourselves for the greater good. Animals do this as a part of everyday life. But we don't necessarily do this as we know better, apparently. We know what's going on we don't need to learn anything as we know it all, you cannot teach us new tricks. How does that sound to you? Is that confidence speaking, or perhaps someone that does know it all, or maybe someone who is fearful that new teachings may get them out of their old, too familiar comfort zone?

Trouble is, animals and nature are continually learning and evolving to a greater depth that we cannot comprehend and, to be honest, to a depth that majority of people don't even see. Where is the evidence? I hear you ask, Well, a very basic example is seen in my back garden. We have a birdbath in our garden that the birds use to bathe and drink from. That was until a week ago when we threw some old stale bread onto the lawn. It was there during one of the hottest days of the summer. The birds being clever stayed out of the sun to a certain extent that meant the bread wasn't eaten and turned into concrete, it was so hard. The following day, I watched a magpie descend on to the lawn and pick up a piece of bread. Well, tried to. It was so hard, he had trouble picking a piece of it up. But pick it up he did, then I saw something quite remarkable. He flew over to the birdbath and dropped the bread into it. He then flew away and sat on the fence and started pruning himself. A short time later, he went over to the birdbath took the now soaked bread out of the water, flew over to the shed and started to eat the bread, that had now softened from its previous hard state. Who on earth taught him how to do that? Well, no one apart from his parents but where did they learn that from? While in Dubai, I was sitting on a sun bed dreaming of all sorts when a crow landed on the sun bed in front of me, it hopped onto the table which had an ice bucket on it. He then proceeded to pick up an ice cube, I thought to cool him or herself down. But no, at that very point another crow appeared and landed on the grass below the first crow. The first crow, now sitting on the sun bed, tilted his/her head to one side and let the ice cube melt into the mouth of the crow on the ground. After a few minutes they swapped the crow on the ground, flew up, picked up the ice cube where the first crow had left it, and then tilted his/her head to let the cold water drop into the mouth of the first crow that was now on the grass. I was fascinated and watched this for ages. They flew off, but again the following day they did the same format. Again, who taught them this? They are simply learning, and although we know they don't have a thinking brain, they have worked out that by doing this they can keep cool. And the magpie back home working out how to turn the hard bread soft. Incredible isn't it that nature does have a way of working things out. She will always find a way and pass this information down to all her subjects including us, but we don't always listen. Unlike the crow and the magpie, if something is taught to us through nature, we have to study it or experiment with it as we don't always take these learnings at face value.

This chapter is about how we learn and what we can take from our life, it's also a little spiritual after all I am a psychic/medium and as such I like to bring some of these teachings to you as well.

Do with these teachings as you will, but as science is now, I feel, coming close to realising that we are more than flesh and blood it takes us deeper down that rabbit hole. It does make me smile when I speak to those that are trying to find that knowing that total inner self. We as humans are experiencing this life on this planet to learn, to understand ourselves from having a human experience. I totally get that, as if we were here knowing all there was, then what would we learn and why would we come here in the first place. We are here to gain experience and to grow. Yes, some can experience and tap into a higher self and a higher way of being, which is a gift, and for some reason, certain people have been given that gift to teach others, a bit like a Satnav here to help and guide people if they go down the wrong route. That in itself should be a learning, you see we are not here to know it all, if we did, then there would be no mystery in life, no questions to ask, in fact no point in life if we did know it all. So, what are we here to learn? Why do most of us drift through life without really learning that thing we came here to learn? Simply because I think we have lost that ability to learn, (I mean really learn about life). I wish I had learned more about 'life and my part in it' at school instead of learning about things like binary that I have never used in the 39 odd years since leaving school. I think learning more about what to expect with life's little ups and downs would have prepared me better. It may have helped me make a bit more sense of the world around me and what to expect. Anyway, I digress, so we think that being human makes us the centre of the universe, which couldn't be further from the truth. Life has been here for over three thousand million years, us around three million and as a modern form of human about 200,000 years. Which means we have only been here around 0.10% of the time, (don't write in, it was an estimate as my calculator cannot work out the correct odds). Therefore, our assumption that we control the earth and everything on it, is a huge miscalculation on our part, as she was doing very well before we came along, and will carry on doing rather well when we are gone. But, as we covered the consciousness and nature part of us earlier in the book, we shall carry on. What is this learning all about? Well I can assure you we are not going to cover Maths or English, but what I would like to do is give you some thought about how we can learn and how we can adapt that learning for the better good. There is the mainstream way of learning, which is the long-term memory, this is the part that retains things like thoughts, interactions, visualisation and feelings among other things, these become connected to the brain when brought into the working memory. As the brain connects these long-term memories into a working memory, it will also add consideration to these selected thoughts. During life this long-term memory works closely with the short-term memory which expands our ideas, feelings and thoughts of past, present and future imagined events. The short-term memory draws from the long-term memory to link prior knowledge and experiences with new understandings. In other words, the short-term memory will try to seek connections with old memories to make new meanings of new ideas, thoughts, feelings, visualisations and link them with understanding from the past, which is why the short-term links with the long term. What this does is limit us, if you think about it, we are continually using past experiences to forge our here and now and our futures, as our brains try to link experiences from the past to get an idea of what we should be thinking now. Now there is another part to this called DIY learning. This occurs when learning environments and conditions engage multiple connections to the brain. As humans, we are more likely to make greater attempts to process and apply new learnings which increases long-term memory and sustained understanding if we explore authentic ways to transfer new ideas and feelings to varied circumstances. In other words, if we look at things as three dimensional instead of two dimensional, like majority of us do, then we could bring various ideas and thoughts to problem solving. The reason why I told you this is so you get an understanding on how thoughts can sabotage us, as thoughts stay above the mind and use past experiences to make sense of new issues and problems that arise now. Even a thought you have about a future plan or idea will also be analysed using a past experience to see if it matches up. I get this, as what the brain/conscious is doing is using logic to try and work things out, and why not. You see the brain doesn't really use logic, if it did it would recognise that the situation or thought or indeed feeling you are in now or that you are thinking about has never actually existed before, nor will it again. So, why use a past experience to make sense of where we are now or something that will happen in the future.

The brain only thinks in what is plausible, in other words it has to think about something in order not to think about it. Let me make that clearer, if I say DO NOT think about a banana, I know you have just thought about it. The brain has to think about something in order not to think about it. That's why when you are trying to give up something for instance sugar treats and you say to yourself, I am not going to have a cookie today. As the mind has to think about not having a cookie, the image of the cookie pops into your mind and you will be thinking about a cookie at a deeper level, even though you don't know you are, that cookie is present in your mind. That's why subliminal advertising works and is now supposedly banned. It uses images and sounds to influence responses in a set audience without the audience being consciously aware of it. To stop that sugar treat, just say to yourself the thought that you want, so say something like 'today I am going to eat and enjoy fruit', that's it, and as the mind thinks about the fruit consciously, the mind has set up an image of some fruit and that's what you will be concentrating on. See, easy, isn't it? The mind will bring you that thing you think about. Another example, you go and buy a car in a colour you don't think there are many of, let's say orange. Then on the way home and days after you see a lot of orange cars that you didn't notice before, why? Because you have set up your mind to see cars painted in orange. Consciously your brain is searching for orange cars and will alert you when it sees one. You can trick your mind into all sorts of things, remember the lemon exercise we did earlier? Did it actually happen? No. Did your mouth salivate as if it were actually happening? Yes. As your brain works in what is plausible and not in logic then as far as the mind knows, you actually put that lemon in your mouth.

I hope that helps in giving you a broad idea about how we think and how the brain and mind can help, but also to sabotage our thinking when we are to navigate through a new or future thought about something we need to focus on. Why do I need to know this? Because it's important to understand how things work so we can look at doing things a little differently, to get that balance more in your favour. As I like to keep things simple, (and to be honest, this isn't complicated) try the following before embarking on a new day just after you wake up, or indeed before you go to bed at night. Say to yourself, *'Today, I am going to let the day run its course, I do not have any pre-set thoughts, ideas about how today will turn out, I understand that what happens to-day has never happened before in my life nor will it happen again.'* Then let it go, by doing that simply saying, you are not tuning in, from an unconscious level, about how today, or if you do it before you go to sleep, tomorrow will turn out. Then as you move through your day, when things happen, just let them, knowing that you have everything you need to deal with that situation as and when it rises. In fact, if you keep that in mind, you will bring that higher subconscious into play knowing that it will help bring the solution as long as you don't get in its way. And that's the problem, we tend to get in its way, by allowing our thoughts of the past to cloud what's happening now by the process we have seen above. How do we let the subconscious help us? Simply by allowing those thoughts and feelings come to us without thinking too much about the process to whatever it is that has come our way. When thinking about a new venture or about something you have planned for tomorrow, think about the end result but don't dwell too much on the journey to get there. You see, you create your reality which creates your life. In fact, there isn't such a thing as reality as that's just your idea about how things should be in your life on this earth. Your version of reality will be different to everyone else's. Don't let that thought of reality get in your way, just ask for a sign each day when thinking about your day ahead and let it come to you. The trick is not to imagine what that sign will look like, as it may be a thought, feeling or some advice you hear someone saying. Just keep an open mind and the answer will come and have some patience, which was one of my biggest challenges, as patience was one of my biggest problems to overcome. This does work and it works well, just as you are thinking that's it, this doesn't work......bingo! The answer comes and the issue or problem seems to resolve itself. Remember though, the answer may come in a way you weren't expecting, that's okay, roll with it as a greater self is at work helping you. If any doubts bring to mind the chapter on the birth of consciousness and recall that we live by the conscious process, but we need to tap into and allow the subconscious to come to us with advice and help. Just some tips and thoughts at how we can sometimes sabotage ourselves and what to do about it when that happens.

As we go through life, I find it encouraging to sit up and take notes on how others learn and adapt to life's challenges, it gives me a sense of the possible through the eye of those that have attempted the impossible and made it work. Take the Hopi Indians for instance, they are experts at desert farming growing corn, squash and beans in the dry desert near Black Mesa, Arizona and have been doing so for generations. How did they succeed where others have failed? They learned years go about keeping moisture-robbing weeds away from their crops and have not known to amend their soil.

They plant in areas that have a more naturally favourably soil and moisture conditions. They grow their corn in clumps of six and spaced well apart so that they conserve water and to mitigate wind damage. They use planting sticks and drop 10 to 12 seeds in one hole, which typically produce around 12 plants, the best six of which are kept growing. They have managed to grow these crops in the high desert where we would have thought that it would be impossible to grow anything. They learned to use the land and to work with its strengths and weaknesses. There is a spiritual side to this as well, the Hopi will not go to the fields unless they have a pure open heart that is filled with hope and love. Remember we are connected to everything and also remember the water experiment we read about in chapter one? If the Hopi are going to the fields with an open and loving heart, then perhaps they are sending this positivity to the crops, as they won't go to the plants when they are feeling negative, so they have learnt the ways of nature and the ways of their spiritual selves. Not bad for a race of people that live in one of the most inhospitable places on earth. This way of living and growing crops has been passed down from generation to generation by the elders and those already working the land. The Amazon tribes of South America have also learned to live and prosper in another, to us, hospitable place on earth, the Amazon rain forests. They too have survived for centuries on the learnings passed down from generations. The children don't go to school, instead once they reach a certain age, they are taught traditions and the ways of the forest from their elders. As I really doubt that learning algebra will help when hunting prey in the forest. They also learn and grow, have spiritual beliefs and work agriculture around the dense forest areas. Other indigenous tribes around the world still live by these teachings and a way of life alien to us, BUT have survived through the centuries. They learn the ways of being and of working with nature and then pass these important messages down to the young. And you know what? It works and has done for a very long time. We come along and try to teach them that our way is best, but is it really? Can you live in the rain forest or in the desert without having a supermarket nearby? Do you know when the seasons are about to change or when a freak weather system is about to hit? No, but they can. When we set out to learn something new, we have to embrace it totally, but also being three dimensional about it. What do I mean? Well okay, we all need the basics of education in our modern society to set us up in life, maths, English, geography, history, etc. But when we learn about life as an adult, we also tried to use that two-dimensional rulebook on how things are, we follow the process of learning, which is good as it follows what everyone else has learned which makes communication easier. How about looking at things from a different perspective? Okay, not so easy with Maths and English, but even then, it can be used to a certain point. What do I mean by three dimensional? I mean seeing the relationships of how things interact with each other. Let's give you an example, the seasons change in the northern hemisphere four times a year, we get spring, summer, autumn and winter. We get to expect the certain temperatures in each season (or at least we get an idea of what the weather will be like) so summer it will be warm, autumn it can be wet and in winter cold and sometimes we get snow. Okay, so that's it. Nothing else to learn, we get our four seasons and expect the weather that will be associated with those seasons. But wait a moment, with those with a three-dimensional outlook, that isn't just it. As the seasons change, we notice how the plants are changing, we see the different birds come and go, we notice what animals in and around where we live change habits and behaviours. We notice some cloud structure changes in the cooler weather, as certain clouds go for a while until atmospheric changes occur to bring them back. Have you notice that in the autumn and winter the song of the Robin is easier to hear than in the summer? This being due to some of our summer visitors departing for warmer climates. Did you notice the swallows leave us to head back to Africa? The basics for most of us is that the grass grows and the hedges need trimming more often in summer. So, when we leave school, we need to be more aware of what we are learning. When I see a client due to the NLP training I have had, I sit in front of him/her and I get to see a three-dimensional image of that person. I just don't sit in front of them and talk small talk in the hope that we engage and do business. I use eye-accessing cues to see how they think, body language to gauge how comfortable they are taking to me, their desk is it messy, clean, tidy, do they have pictures on their desks if so what of? These are all levels of information used to gauge information about that person. And then once I gather that information, I can make very quick decisions and choices of how I interact with that person. It's that three-dimensional outlook we need to take note in all we do. Bring in that higher subconscious self into play, by allowing it to guide and help you and to point out things along the way you may have missed. Use those gut feelings and just let go of the two-dimensional outlook by NOT dismissing a gut feeling or by dismissing something that may look a little out of place. Learn to use the signals being presented to you, it really will open up a world that you may have dismissed in the past. Three-dimensional thinking is just allowing yourself to look outside of the normal and to engage with the things around you by looking at them in a different way. Understand them, don't just take it as 'that's just the way it is'. Two plus two is four, but just because it's autumn doesn't mean IT'S JUST AUTUMN, look at it closer, see the PH balance in the soil alter as the leaves change colour and eventually fall to the ground. Notice the birds storing more food, in fact the noise of local birds as the summer visiting birds migrate back to warmer climates. Notice behaviour changes in animals, even your domestic pet will have a slight behaviour change, if you take the time to notice. When learning something new, take time to really understand it by looking beyond what the eyes and conscious is telling you. Use the higher self to allow you to understand and to see the relationships we have with what it is we need, or are learning. Another example, when I say, 'Who are you?', you may say your name, height, what you do for a job, your family structure, where you live, what you like and dislike, your birth sign perhaps. Okay great, but that's a little two dimensional, as we don't spend much time really looking at ourselves. Now I want you to describe you through the 'eyes of someone else. What would they see and how would they describe you? They would probably go more in depth about your personality, funny things about how you walk, how you eat your food etc. You see, we look at others in a more detailed in-depth way then we see ourselves. Take time to look at you, it can be quite fun and also a little enlightening to see you as you. Go on try it, make it fun you will be surprised when you see yourself in a more three-dimensional way.

This looking at yourself can be used in the sports arena, I have worked successfully with golfers who want to understand why their game, at times, goes a little squiffy. It's a great levelling tool for all sports people and I have also used it with footballers. The idea is to get them to see themselves make that swing or play that shot etc., from a disassociated point of view. i.e. see it from someone else's eyes. How do we do that? Well, we get them to play the shot, feel it, sense it get them to close their eyes so they can engage with it. Next we get them to physically stand in another position (the second position) away from where they took that shot and get them to point out in their view what went wrong. We then get them back into the (first position) and to listen to that advice. Then get them to try it and see if that advice works. If needed, repeat the process if necessary. What we are doing is getting them to look at the complete picture instead of the two dimensional one they were working with. You can use this in all manner of topics from the sports arena to the office, to out selling. What we are doing here is just getting yourself to see yourself and giving yourself some advice on how it may work better. Try it and again remember to have fun with it. This isn't complicated, just another tool to help you get out of your way and to learn something new.

One thing that may be holding you back from learning is our old friend the ego. That part of us that says that we don't need to learn we know it all, what could I possibly know more? Let's just quickly remind ourselves what the ego does and doesn't do, as a better understanding can help you understand and learn more about you. So, what is the ego? The simple truth is, it holds you back and puts your mind in a place where that part of you says I don't need to know any more I know it all. It also puts you in to thinking that things are NOT possible or at least it tricks you into thinking that. The ego is fuelled by so many things in our lives which include our life stories, memories, achievements or lack of them. Our possessions, the media, how we see a challenge, what we look like, in fact the list is endless. It's basically that part of us that builds upon the negatives of our lives and how we think. The ego is always trying to make us happy as it centres its attention on obtaining something or someone to make you happy and when it doesn't get it, it brings on unhappiness. When you realise that being happy has nothing to do with obtaining that thing or someone, but more about who you are, then the ego begins to let go and you will begin to find that happiness. The ego will always try and build and build and build, and while it's doing that, it will never be happy or at peace, and guess what? Neither will you. People who live their lives purely by the ego will never be happy and will probably be shallow, easily upset, depressed, angry and generally moody and, well, that's just the good points.

So that's it, nothing complicated about it, but how do you let go and stop living your life from the ego? One thing to remember is that a properly managed ego is a good thing, but you need to let go of its gravitational pull and let it work for you, rather than you, work for it. Nothing you are thinking about, except what you are reading on this page, is important right now. So, open your mind, there is nothing that you need to think about feel or see. Just open your mind and let it all go, then take a deep breath and relax. How does that feel? Having not to think about anything right now! Good, isn't it? Perhaps empowering, perhaps a light feeling in your mind, perhaps feeling tired. That's good, well done if you do, or any other feeling you have that gives you that sense of being free. So now you have disengaged the ego see it for what it is, which is only a force within you making you feel incomplete. I bet you would like that idea and feeling of being released from that gravitational pull toward unhappiness and instead being pulled toward greater happiness, possibilities and miracles?

Let's look at things differently here for a while, especially now your mind is free from 'wanting'. What life offers at every step and at every opportunity is the chance to grow, to be at a higher level of consciousness and you can only be that way if you let go of what you 'think' is right for you and just simply learn from every part of your life at every minute. I don't mean analysing everything at every moment, but when something happens look at it as a gift. Let's try something here, think back to a time when something happened, something that at the time you didn't like. Now stop, forget the old feeling of anger or helplessness, whatever it is you felt, and now look at it from a different angle, from a disassociated point of view. What can you learn from that time, don't look at it from a point of view of what happened. Instead ask yourself what I can learn from that time, about how I reacted, was it the ego acting or me. I bet it was your ego, so now, how would you would have reacted if you take that ego away, when you remained calm and took a lesson out of the situation instead of reacting to it. I bet if you do this properly you will feel empowered, strong minded and even perhaps calm and in control. If that's the case, then you are using your higher intelligence to see things for what they are, not what your ego thinks they are. If you are in control, then you will deal with things easily without fuss or stress. When you look back later at that situation, it will just be a memory nothing more nothing less, but the fear and worry attached to that situation will have gone. All the ego does is bridge that gap between what it thinks reality is and your personal identity. Like most things it doesn't exist, only in the part of us that says it exists, simply because we have let it grow within our psyche. However, it serves no purpose and, to be honest, has no purpose, apart from making you miserable and leaving you with that hopeless feeling. Let it go, get rid of it. Would you keep a weed in your prize flowerbed just because you think it serves a purpose? No, you would dig it up and get rid of it. So why let this weed in the guise of your ego grow within you? As it serves no purpose. At least a weed may look pretty when it flowers, whereas the ego remains ugly and dull. I hope this gives you a brief idea of what the ego does and how you can overcome this part of you. It's been growing ever since you had that conscious awareness when you were young, when that false realisation came into your being that you need to grab life before someone else grabs it. Recognise it when it comes into your daily life and then use common sense to make you sit up and realise that life doesn't need to be 'grabbed' it's there you just need to associate with it.

I like to think, this chapter has made you aware that we need to let go of our ego's and by purely engaging with the subconscious, which is your higher self, it can bring great learning's about yourself and your environment. Some ancient traditions are still using this today, and along with being three dimensional and connecting to nature, still manage to do things that we cannot understand. Along with this they continue to practice it and pass it down to the younger generations, who I hope will do so with their children and their children's children. Let's not lose these amazing wise and wonderful old ways of being that are still so very needed today.

Chapter Eleven
Ancient Ways of the Shaman

Why are the ways of the Shaman part of a book about being a human whisperer? Because I feel they are an important part of the past and possibly the future, with their wisdom and their knowledge of us, as humans. Science is now catching on fast with regard to acknowledging that there is a lot of evidence to back up the workings and thoughts of these wonderful people. As this book is to open up the imagination and gives some insights into how we can make our world a better place for us and for those around us, then I believe that the ways of the Shaman are important. Plus, it satisfies my spiritual side.

What is a shaman and why do I feel they are important to our way of life? Simply as they do what I am hoping this book will do, and that is, to take you to a place and time that is parcel to our place and time, where I feel we need to go if we are to survive the next few hundred years. We shall cover that a little later in more depth, but for now let's see what a shaman is and what do they, or what they can provide. Where did it all begin? Shaman practices can trace their roots back to around 12,000 years ago, with early records show it was traced back to the Ural Mountains and most probably from the Tugus tribal people. The word shaman has its origins from an Indian word meaning to 'heal oneself' and applies to a person that practices their art of healing for the common good of their tribe, or people. They go through an initiation period, which may take a few years, before they become or are recognised as a shaman. A shaman may not be from the same family, although the 'knowledge' can be passed down the family line. A shaman is a person that is regarded to have influence in the realms of good and bad spirits. They are active in the areas of North America, Northern Asia, and here in Europe. These people heal through ritual, and, what I am interested in is the use of deviation. In case you haven't come across the word deviation, it means *the practice of seeking knowledge of the future of the unknown, by supernatural means.* Sounds scary, doesn't it? But actually it's not, it's just what we have covered in this book, remember we are connected to everything and anything, so what the shamans do is to tap into this unseen energy. How? Well, in our modern life we get sick and then we get healed by medicine created by science, i.e. antibiotics etc. When ancient people and people to-day get sick and call on a shaman or medicine man, the way of healing is more based on a placebo effect, where the patient thinks they are being healed and that induces the healing process. The interesting part is that the shaman can bring on this effect on their patient which science has witnessed and studied, but yet doesn't really understand how the shaman actually does this and get the results they do. It has to do with engaging with the patient at a higher level and engaging with them using this quantum energy, which to some outsiders can look as if they are engaging with the supernatural but in fact just using good old Mother Nature. This is one of the things we have lost in our modern day lives, that ability to tap into Mother Nature, which we covered earlier in the book. However, what is refreshing to me is that we haven't completely lost this ability to use nature to heal us, as long as we still have shamans out there to carry on this practice. You never know, in time we may all be able to tap into this realm. Can you imagine ringing up your local doctor's surgery and get asked, "Would you like to see Dr Smith or the Shaman?"

"I know which one I will go and see."

So how do shamans actually tap into this energy soup? Yet again we find that there is a correlation between the shaman and modern-day physics. You see the shaman taps into the unseen energy field and sees the world as a set of vibrations, which is exactly what quantum physics has also discovered, that we vibrate, as does everything around us. To explain further, science has discovered that everything vibrates and has an inherent probability vibrational pattern, this enables physicists to work out the very structure of atoms and molecules and how these particles emit and absorb electromagnetic energy. It appears that the shamans have understood this for thousands of years and yet only now do we have the right equipment to discover this phenomenon. Shamans can tap into and understand this vibrational force that surrounds us and is a part of us. It's been discovered that shamans have an ability to tap into this field and by doing so alter it to a higher healing vibrational state and by doing so, brings healing to the patient in question. They do this in several ways, one is by chanting and using like a white noise to raise the vibrational energy around the person they are working with. Which brings me to an experience I had when I was a young boy of around 14 years of age. I was, (reluctantly it has to be said), taken to a monastery in the south of the UK by my parents for an outing, mainly to buy some of the local honey and mead they made at this wonderful place. Mead, by the way, is an alcoholic drink made from honey and herbs which was a speciality of this particular monastery. I asked if I could have a wander around to which my parents agreed, after all it was a safe and secure place. After a while I came across the chapel and was stopped in my tracks by this incredible noise. At 14 years of age, I was already aware of being psychic and I was aware of things around me but nothing prepared me for this angelic noise which I was confronted with. The noise came from the chapel and was being made by a number of monks chanting, it was just the most amazing sound I had ever heard. I had not heard Gregorian chanting before and it was the most incredible sound. The monks were practicing and the door to the chapel just slightly open, I am not sure whether it was by design or mistake that the door had been left ajar. Either way, I found myself routed to the spot, it was in a very old monastery and the sound from the chanting just filled the air and echoed around the fine old structure. Then something happened to me, my view of the world began to change, the stark brown and whitewashed walls of the area I was standing in began to change colour and became a soft yellow hue, my vision became blurred and softer, I became lightheaded and I felt myself swaying. The strange thing was, this all felt normal and almost welcoming, I wasn't scared in fact I became peaceful and calm. All too soon, the singing stopped and I felt my head cloud over as I realised the brown and white-washed walls had returned, my body felt heavy as I became nauseous and I staggered a bit. Two monks appeared from the chapel saw me and kindly escorted me back to my parents. I didn't understand what had happened to me, but I loved what it brought me, that deep and penetrative calm and peace I had never experienced before. It wasn't until a few years later I was invited to attend a Druid ceremony where their shaman started chanting during the proceedings and guess what? The same thing happened to be then as it did in the monastery. My surrounding became softer, more colourful and my head became light, as I felt that peace and tranquillity return, the same as it did when I was listening to the monks. Now as quantum physics understand we are energy and are connected to this energy soup that vibrates and moves, so was the chanting by the monks and that of the shaman, (two different styles of chanting) able to affect by my energy by lifting it to a higher state? I didn't ask the others at the Druid session at the time if they felt the same, as I was so engrossed in my own experience. I did ask some of the group a little while afterwards what they got from the ceremony, some of them described what I had felt, even though at that time, I didn't disclose what I had experienced. Did the shaman in that session and the Gregorian chants I experienced at the monastery manage to raise my vibrational state? The immense peace and calm I felt at both of those times along with the colours in the room becoming brighter and yet softer was incredible, perhaps my body and mind had been opened ready for healing? Is that what happens when a shaman manipulates and raises the vibrational state of their patient? All I can say is, if that is the case then I can understand why healing takes place.

Shamans understand the connections of everything to anything and also understand things like totem animals which we covered earlier in the book. It's kind of interesting when you think that they have known this for thousands of years, yet we are only understanding it now thanks to modern science. In science there is a thing called non-locality which is where an action taking place here can instantly affect actions taking place over there. As this has to do with quantum mechanics and is a little complicated for this book, I will leave that here for you to do some of your own research as it is quite in depth. There are some great books on the subject that explain it better than I can, from people like Dr Fred Allen Wolf a particular favourite of mine. But again, what really interests me is that these shaman's, these workers of nature, know and understand this and have done so for generation upon generation of teaching. Anyway again I digress, so, shamans recognise noise and the fact noise vibrates, which then flows down through that connectivity that connects us to everything around us and by doing so, brings more energy into our bodies and minds which invites healing to take place. This also taps into what I was mentioning earlier that as a medium and psychic, I can also tap into a person's energy field to read how they are feeling and, in certain respects, what they are thinking. I don't use sound or chanting but perhaps I will try this as well and see if I can start to induce the same kind of healing a shaman can bring; I will let you know how I get on. How does this vibration help to cure a dysfunction within a human or animal? Theory time, so the vibrations of this earth we call home, are connected and have a common bond with our vibrations as we are related. We, during our lives and during times of stress and upsets can unbalance the vibrational signature of the cells of our bodies. I believe the shaman using vibrational energy can bring about healing by bringing the cells in our bodies back into vibrational alignment with each other. Is the healing taking place using non-locality as an action, taking place here, i.e. raising the vibrational energy around a patient, thus causing the vibration of the cells in that body over there, to become instantly aligned with the universal energy that is surrounding it, thus promoting harmony? I was chatting to a shaman who advised me that this vibration is connected to the different parts of the body and amazingly, he can tell which part of the body is not in line due to the different way it vibrates. What he does is try to re-align this part of the body with nature to rebalance this vibration to what it should be like under normal healthy vibration. I know modern medicine will say that's nonsense, is it? Why has this stuff been used for thousands of years and worked? But now we put our trust into man-made medicine, which I understand has its place, and I think any dysfunction should be run by a doctor first. But, perhaps modern medicine and the old ways of healing may work side by side? I am going to say something here that may get me into trouble. I don't really think that we will ever go back to the old ancient ways, why? Because the pharmaceutical industry is worth billions of pounds, dollars whatever. Could you imagine if we all started going to see the shaman or medicine man and not the doctor, and not take modern-day drugs? The collapse of some of these industries would also see the collapse of some economies, something I think will never be allowed to happen. Anyway, let's go back to the subject in hand. The vibrational points used by a shaman has a similar property and working with another ancient practice that of Reiki, so I will use an extract from my first book to show the similarities. Reiki is a form of healing that is actually becoming popular once again, and I have experienced this first-hand and it works, really works. I had a bad left shoulder for months, it was getting me down as I couldn't get to the gym and it just niggled me every time I tried to do something. I went to see a Reiki practitioner (her name is Kelly, I am sure she wouldn't mind me telling you her name as she is brilliant) As soon as I walked into the room, I felt a sense of calm and confidence. She looked at me smiled and after taking come general notes on my health asked me to stand up and looked at my body. At this time, I hadn't actually said it was my shoulder, but she looked at me told me to sit down, came around behind me and just put her hands above my left shoulder. She didn't touch me but just hovered her hands above me, kept them there for a while, then told me to go home have a bath in some Dead Sea salts, which I could get from the supermarket and see how I went. I didn't feel anything had changed after my session, but I followed her instructions. Yes, you guessed it the following morning I woke up, got up had breakfast then it dawned on me my shoulder felt a lot easier. A few days later the stiffness and pain had completely gone. Not only that, it never returned. Coincidence? I am not sure, but something else, that first night after my session I had the best night's sleep I have had for months. What did it cost me to get my shoulder right £25.00? I had spent over £200.00 going to traditional forms of healing and nothing, £25.00 and a half hour session with a spiritual healer, sorted! As I mentioned earlier, it's subjective, it worked for me but I have an open mind about such things. That may be the basis of a lot of it, having an open mind. I think having that open mind allows you to be subjective and in doing so, allows the greater universal forces to work with your mind and body. Whereas having a closed mind, which a lot of us allow to happen due to outside influences, stops that universal force from coming in and helping us. Reiki was founded back in the 1800s in Japan by a Buddhist monk named Mikao Usui. He was asked about the healing that Jesus did during his early days while at school. So, he set out to find the answer to that question and while on a meditation and fasting quest he felt a great energy enter his body. He then used this energy in directing it to people with ailments, it seemed to work, and the rest is history, as they say. This type of healing is becoming more and more popular as people try to find an alternative to traditional medicines and therapies. I have seen the greatest of sceptic's melt, when their condition gets better in the practice of alternative therapies.

How does this dysfunction come into play in the first place, I mean why are we not fit and healthy all the time? Why does our bodies become out of kilter, we are in nature all the time, so surely, she must be giving us that good vibrational energy all the time? Well, the answer as you probably already know is that nature continually gives us this good vibrational energy, but we counteract it with negative thoughts, negative feelings, fear and other emotions that block that all import energy from coming to us. The result is that the body becomes dysfunctional and the weakest and prone parts of our bodies react by becoming out of vibrational pattern with the rest of our bodies and the energy that surrounds us. That's all it takes is a negative thought, as remember our minds/brains are the engine part of our being. The body simply reacts to what it is being told by how we think and act. A simple negative thought is all it takes to start this dysfunction with a certain part of our bodies. A negative thought won't necessarily have the impact to start this negative process, for instance if a car cuts you up on the road you get upset, annoyed perhaps, but then after a short while the average person will move on and it's in the past. If we keep telling a negative story about ourselves, we start to believe it, we start to become that story and that's when our bodies start to react to this thought. How? Because we start to push that negative energy into our bodies, we become that thing we tell ourselves. I am also a great believer that modern stress and anxiety are the biggest culprits to us becoming dysfunctional. We, as humans, were never designed to keep that constant stress and anxiety in our bodies. It's a very basic emotion it was there when we were living in caves and had a very simple knowledge of the outside world. It is our fight or flight response that kicks in when we face danger. The blood leaves our internal organs and moves out to our limbs ready to fight that thing or run away from it. At the same time the body releases hormones into our system, adrenalin and noradrenalin which increases heart rate and blood pressure. Once the danger has passed the body returns to a state of balance or homeostasis and we carry on as normal. However, present-day work, life etc. keep us in a state of flight or flight for longer. We find that life itself is stressful and so the body does what the mind tells it to do and is constantly releasing stress hormones into our bodies, which over a period of time can cause long term damage. I am not sure why life is like that, we have everything we can possibly want, there is an abundance of everything, yet we want more. Life becomes fast paced as we work longer, helped by technology which means we can constantly interact with the work environment. I have at work, four ways that someone can contact me, actually five if you include the good old telephone. When I am at home, I can check e-mails, interact with head office through an internal communication channel, get texts, WhatsApp messages, life is great I can keep on top of work. Yea right! Anyway, life these days is, for some, a constant battle trying to keep calm, positive and subjective. How can we stop these negative thoughts? Let me explain first about why we attract them, yes, we attract them, it's all our fault. In my first book, I talk briefly about the power of attraction. How what we want is immediately pushed out into the universe for grandfather to provide it. (I call the universe Grandfather as it gives it a tangible and something I can relate to)

What we want, either negative or positive is always pushed out into the universe for grandfather to provide, and remember, the mind only works in what's plausible, it doesn't work in logic. The problem is we spend far too much time thinking about that thing we don't want and then as the universal law works, the universe will bring you that thing you don't want, as at a conscious level you are continually looking for it. The personal conscious doesn't know if that thing you are searching for is a good thing or a bad thing, as it works at that non-judgemental level, it simply brings you what you are looking for. If that thing you are looking for is fear based or stress based etc. then you will get it. How many of you have that horrible journey to work each morning and night? That job that you can change if you like and really wanted to, but you don't as it becomes familiar, it becomes who you are. Guess what? Yes, that stress and anxiety is also part of that package but is hidden in that part that says yes it's okay, its familiar, it's what I have to do, until one day, bang! You get a warning shot as the body becomes out of balance, you ignore it until something more serious happens in your body. You see the doctor who says change your lifestyle, you don't of course as this lifestyle is who you are and then something more serious happens. This also works with the thing you want; it's the same process you want something you focus on it you send that message out and eventually it comes to you. Maybe not in the way you were expecting, but it does come to you. We can sometimes sabotage that thing we want but denying that we want it, or that perhaps it's out of our reach, and guess what, Grandfather responds by saying, 'oh, that thing you want, you want it out of your reach, okay then' and then it remains out of your reach. The trick is putting energy into that thing you want by expressing it as much and as often as you can, but not by saying I want that, but by simply saying 'thank you' for that thing and having the good feelings about whatever it is you want. Don't waste energy longing and looking for it, just accept that it will be yours. Don't think with lack, think with thanks for whatever it is you desire. Quantum physics understands this process through transitional thinking. It's all about pathways connecting the process of wanting that thing to a connection with having that thing. If you say, 'I want that thing', BUT the connection with wanting that thing 'becomes dysfunctional due to you simply stating, yes but it's beyond my grasp then there is an imbalance. You wanting that thing becomes confused with you saying 'ah yes but it's beyond me' as then grandfather will keep it from your grasp. What you need to do is say, "I want that thing and I know it will come to me." That's it. Don't complicate things, let your desire grow by always believing it is coming to you. Always try to keep the balance by asking for that thing and then knowing it is coming to you. That way the thing you desire will come to you quickly and as mentioned maybe not in the way you think it will, but it will come, it's the law. Just keep in mind when the genie in Aladdin says, "Be careful what you wish for."

That was a huge digression from the topic of shamans but I wanted to point out to you why our bodies can become dysfunctional and why it is important to focus on the thing you want rather than the thing you don't, simply by focusing on the receiving of that thing you desire. I think this is important hence the need to cover this. The shamans know all this and when you go to see one the first thing, they may do is just go over a history of your past, they will then know exactly what part of the body may need healing. Shamans have a great sense of us, and by us I mean humans. For a long time now I have always seen the body as an extension of us, of our minds who we are, nature. I thought I may be on the wrong path as mostly everyone else thinks of the body as a machine, some even think the body is us, they don't think that something maybe driving it. And as we think like that, then thinking also becomes two-dimensional, it lacks substance and imagination. If we lose that ability to become three-dimensional and open to realising there is a subconscious, a higher part to us all, then we lose that ability to create, as we close ourselves down to thinking that we, our bodies are all there is. The shaman opens this and understands that this western way of thinking is causing the dysfunction of ourselves and our bodies, as that vibrational pull, brings in negative energy and thoughts into our being. This is not only known by the shaman, but medicine men/woman all over the planet from the North American Indian to the Buddhist and ancient traditions of Ayurvedic practice. I believe, that in order for the western world to start to heal itself, it/we have to take responsibility for our own actions. Open and realise, as we saw in chapter two, that we are a part of the greater universe and that this universe (grandfather) will supply everything we want, be it negative or positive. Let's start to think positively and realise we have everything we need, we don't have to think of negatives. I understand that negativity has a place in our world alongside the positive. We do not know what the positive is, unless we have that negative, it is like a pointer to where we should be rather than where we are. The negative is just that a pointer, it doesn't have to become a part of who you are.

There is a part to the shaman and old practices of healing which I am not entirely comfortable with and, to be honest, I am not sure why this still happens and that is the use of hallucinogenic. In the past, the medicine man would use these, from a mixture of herbs and other substances passed down through the generations. This is to entice a dreamlike state into the patient, where the shaman/ medicine man can then bring on this higher vibrational state. Now if I can get into this altered state by listening to monks or a shaman chanting then I am not sure this hallucinated stimulus is really necessary. Perhaps, it gives the patient a feeling of a higher self or that the medicine being practised is working thus causing the placebo effect. What I will say is that we can get into that state very easily by meditating or even light hypnotherapy without the need for an outside influence from a herb or some kind of drug. I could be completely wrong, and I may have missed the point, but if nature can produce this kind of state without a narcotic stimulant then I am not sure why we would need one. After all, we are bound only by our imagination. Anyway, just a thought I would put out there and see what you think.

Moving on, is it possible we can bring back the way of the shaman into our western world? Can we re-tap into that world that once we were capable of, but has since been forgotten? Can we heal ourselves like we did years ago? I listened to a radio program the other day and they were saying that things like cancer, stress and AIDS are the scourge of our modern day lives. Why? I know they had cancer in ancient Egyptian times as some of the mummified bodies showed they had cancer in certain forms. But, did the older generations know how to heal themselves and have a belief in the healing process that the body could heal itself? Were the use of the older traditions of the Shaman, medicine men and Ayurvedic practices more effective in older times, as people had faith in the process? I think we need to look more closely at these older traditional ways of healing and being. They have been around for thousands of years and perhaps if we can only change and challenge how we interact with nature and have a better understanding of how healing actually takes place, then our thinking will also change and perhaps we can start to work with nature and our inner subconscious to bring balance back to our bodies and minds. The fact of healing is a mind-set of potential and possibilities. Let me leave you with this thought before we move onto the next chapter on imagination. As we see ourselves as conscious matter, we allow ourselves to follow a set pattern, one that has been built up over a period of physical time. As these patterns ebb and flow, we, who deal with this consciousness on a daily basis, are only seeing or realising a small part of the process. With this limited capacity and restricted self-image, we have limited ideas to the magic of our own bodies. To be able to release those magical properties, that the shaman understands, we need to be aware of our ability to self-heal using the traditional ideas and thoughts that we are bigger than just us. We are part of a bigger universe that moves and flows through us and within us at all times. Bringing back that vibrational balance will in itself cause equilibrium to exist in our bodies. Understand the western idea that we cannot heal ourselves without medication. Yes, we may at times need medication but don't become dependent on it, try alternatives and look at the bigger picture that outside influences may be causing you to become ill. Walk with the shaman and be the universe, as casting aside everything else, being a part of the universe is what we are, what we have been and what we will always be.

Chapter Twelve
Imagination

The last chapter was just an eye opener into the world of the shaman and to get you thinking of other possibilities that are out there in the world which leads onto this chapter on the imagination. What do I mean by imagination? I am not talking about the 80s pop group! I am talking about that part of us that creates the world around us. Actually, this chapter is about more than the imagination it is also about thought. Most of us have thoughts, in fact it is estimated by experts that we have between sixty and eighty thousand thoughts a day, every day that's around 2,100 thoughts an hour. That's a lot of thinking, gosh, no wonder we are mentally tired. I mentioned in the last chapter that if we desire something and if we look at that thing positively then it will come to us, as that's the law. However, can you imagine trying to think positively on something and also bombarding your mind with eight thousand other thoughts? That's why clarity is needed when thinking about that thing you desire. Spend time each day, morning, afternoon, evening, night etc. just giving thanks for that desire, be clear about it and never let judgement enter your mind.

Can we help the healing process of our bodies and minds by imagination? The answer is, yes and as we saw before, the shaman can raise the vibrational energy and by us visualising, we can probably help the process. Why? As we saw earlier, the mind doesn't know what is real and what is imaginable. It will react to the stimulus as if that thing is happening or not. Remember the exercise with the lemon we did in an earlier chapter? The thought of putting a lemon in your mouth made your mouth salivate. Did you really do it? No, but the mind thinks you did. That is just using the power of the imagination. Here is an interesting thought, the body responds to the mind, it's the engine room and so why wouldn't it? However, the body gives the mind physical boundaries as we believe we are bound by what we can physically do. As a result, the mind thinks within boundaries and around the wheel we go, we think we can, the mind says yes, the body says 'ah! But hold on, I am not capable of that' so the mind says, okay, so we are bound by what we cannot do. That's another interesting thought, isn't it? We are bound by what we cannot do. What if we can project our minds to saying that really, we are capable of anything and not listen to the body? What if we can tap into that vibrational energy and change our physicality to be able to achieve anything we want? Wouldn't that be something worth pursuing? For sure but how? It has to start with that self-sabotage we all put ourselves through, by believing that this is it, there isn't anything else, we have a mind and a body and that's it, that's the old two-dimensional thinking coming into play again. Remember, we are more than what you see in the mirror, we have a subconscious, we are connected to everything and anything. Realistically if you wanted to become a tiger it's impossible as we don't have the same DNA as a tiger that would allow us to walk on four legs have huge teeth and claws. But we can understand that tiger for what it is for what they represent. If you can get into the mind of a tiger, which a lot of researchers do, then you can start to think like one. Would you become that physical tiger? No, would you understand and become the spiritual side of a tiger? Yes, why not? It's only your imagination and what you think you are, or not, capable of that is holding you back from understanding that tiger or whatever it is you want to become. There are interesting stories of humans that have been brought up by monkeys or wolves. These people still have two legs and two arms, they stand upright and walk, but they take the spirit of that animal into their being, and in all intense and purposes they are that animal. One poor sole in Spain, Mr Marcos Rodríguez Pantoja, was adopted by a pack of wolves when he was stranded in Spain's Sierra Morena mountain range, aged seven, and was found living in a cave and brought back to civilisation when he was 19. Was he a human? Yes, did he live and work with the wolves as if he was a member of the pack? Again, the answer is yes. We have to educate ourselves in not living within the boundaries we set ourselves. We have to look further than that, we can do so by using our imaginations into a conscious thought, that anything is possible. Using the imagination is or was one of the senses we used to have which worked alongside the usual five which is what we hear, see, touch, taste and smell. It's not all lost, some expert oenologist's or coffee or tea blenders can still use this imagination then they are tasting or smelling. They can smell or taste the different components to whatever it is they are testing and then by using their imaginations they can smell lavender, or toffee, chocolate or liquorice, whatever it is they can pick up. However, that is not open to a lot of people who just say, "Oh yes, I smell coffee, or tea, or yes, that's wine," very frustrating as if we engage that sixth part to our senses, we can open up a world of different experiences. As a psychic, I can engage with the building or area I am in, I am able to smell, hear and sometimes taste the area around me. For instance, I was in Tintern Abbey a while ago and while walking around these ancient ruins, I suddenly smelt incense wafting around one side of the site. I looked around to see if a candle or some kind of incense sticks were burning but there wasn't any, so this was me tapping into what the Abbey might have been like. I stopped and closed my eyes letting my imagination blend with the surroundings and the smell of the incense. I found myself looking at a majestic image of what it may have looked like many years ago when it was a working monastery. I have done this many times and once while in a famous cafe in London's West End. I walked in and was hit by a smell that, to be honest, smelt of damp with a mixture of cheap perfume. I sat closed my eyes and was met by a spirit called George who took me back to what this area looked like back in the 1800s. I took a mental image wrote it down and did some research a little later. I was astonished, as where the people I told and described the room to, as the images we found matched exactly what George had showed me and to which I made notes of. What some people call the sixth sense, I simply call it part of the senses we all have, if we only allow the imagination to come into play and let it be a part of our everyday experience. It does worry me that with all the technology, phones, games, tablets and laptops etc. are we taking away the power of the imagination from the children and future generations? We in the western world, see the body as a mechanical part of who we are, but it isn't, it is a part of the life around us and exists with that life at every level. Start to realise that you have an active imagination which produces thoughts about your world. If you can start to bring this awareness into your daily routine, then you start to open your mind to new leanings about what is real. A lot of what we are to learn while on this planet we call home, actually comes from the imaginary realm. It's just we don't trust it, as we are taught that such things we see as kids like imaginary friends, fairies and angels are all a part of our vivid imaginations they don't really exist. Really? They don't exist? So if they don't exist, why do we read Holy Scriptures that talk about such things Archangel Michael, Archangel Gabriel? People say oh yes, they are in the bible and work with God. Good, excellent, then why when a child comes home and says he has seen an angel at the bottom of the garden is he treated with such ridicule? Children at an early stage are not blinded and confused with the modern world. They, to some extent, are in this imaginary realm the same realm where medicine men and shamans go to when they heal people. That same realm where Jesus worked from and where God is said to reside. The same realm that I use when working with the spirit world. What happens is that we say to the children, "Oh that's nice but they don't really exist."

Oh okay, then. They go to Sunday school or church where they learn about these angels and probably get very confused about it all. Why wouldn't an innocent child that hasn't been bamboozled by age and teachings that says that they are nothing except flesh and blood, be able to tap into the imaginary realm where we all came from and where we will all return to? Why wouldn't they be able to see things that most adults cannot? Probably that as we become adults, we have this basic survival instinct that says I am being threatened. What happens then is we focus only on the foreground of our lives and the background becomes fuzzy and lost. It's that background that we must bring back into focus if humankind is to survive any length of time on this planet. If we can change how we perceive ourselves from that 'I must survive mentality' to one that accepts there is a part of our world that majority don't even know exists, then we change our perception of who we are. How would we do that? We have to change the understanding of how and what we observe, as that creates the reality we see ourselves in. If you can change the 'how' then we can change the 'what'; change how you see, and importantly what you think about yourself, and you change what is actually present in the world. It's that observer affect we covered earlier. What you perceive not only affects you, it also affects the object of your perception by what you believe is out there. There is a teaching from ancient scripts written about the time Jesus was said to have been on this planet, as even at that point they knew a thing or two about the law of what we call 'reality'. If we look at these teachings from all these years ago, perhaps Jesus was the first real Metaphysicist? I will add that I am not being blasphemous here, I am simply looking at this in an objective point of view. If Jesus was the first to explore and bring the teachings of God or the universe into our daily lives, then a lot of his teaching in the new and old scriptures fall into what metaphysics is also telling us. For an example, Jesus talked about 'for out of the abundance of the heart the mouth speaketh' he was talking about the power of words, and that whatever was in our hearts we expressed. That's interesting because whatever is in our hearts, is that what we are at that point. What do I mean by that? Well, if we feel fear, anxiety, angry, or indeed pleasure or love, this will be expressed in the words and actions we use. Jesus, I feel, knew what studiers of metaphysics know now, which is that emotions create energy and energy creates matter. It's the universal law, it is how it works. In other words, we are what we think, we bring forth to us that, which we think and feel, which we have already covered. I believe that Jesus knew of this universal law that God or the universe, which ever you believe created our world, used and projected onto us through the teachings of Jesus. I also feel and think that at the time Jesus was walking around, these ideas were a little too advanced for most people to get their minds around, after all if people now living in the 21st century are struggling with it, how would you expect people living two thousand years ago to understand it? Jesus knew how the power of healing worked and he knew about the powerful nature of that thing we now call Metaphysics. Let's cover that area for a while, as at this stage I think it is important to understand this theory. What is metaphysics? According to the encyclopaedia it is as follows: ***Metaphysics, the philosophical study whose object is to determine the real nature of things.*** It comes from Greek word's meaning 'beyond nature'. In other words, beyond that physical reality. As we saw earlier, it is how thought creates energy and it's that energy that creates matter, it's the universal law and cannot ever be changed. How does that translate into our daily lives? Simply, that thoughts become things. During our daily lives we make guesses, have thoughts, ideas, make assumptions and make plans born from unrealistic possibilities, which are driven by false information we give ourselves from information we pick up second-by-second, minute-by-minute, hour-by-hour and so on. The one true thought we should remember is exactly that, it is thought that creates our personal and collective world, which we covered earlier in the book. Couple that with emotion and the universe goes about creating that in the physical world.

What you think about the world around you, the events in your life and other people, will and does control YOUR life. Put into context what you think you will get. Think you are being picked on you will be picked on. Think you have poor health, guess what? You will get poor health. Likewise think you are healthy, you will become healthy, think you are loved and it will attract love to you.

If you believe you have no control over your destiny, then you won't control your destiny. Anything that happens reinforces this mind-set that you are not in control, and it becomes deeply embedded into your psyche that someone else controls your future. Everything that happens to you is a product of what your beliefs are about yourself. If you think that at every corner there is someone ready to trip you up, then at every corner someone will be there ready to do just that. Whatever prediction you say about yourself will come true, it is the universal law. Your life in this world is simply created around the products of your own making, that what you, and you only, think and believe. This may be brought on by outside influences, but your life is and will always be a product of your choosing. We are the creators of our own life and those circumstances within it. It amuses me when people say, "Ah, I cannot believe that thing I asked for didn't come to me." In almost every case, it is a simple case of not asking, for whatever it is that you desire, in the right way.

We say to the universe/God, *Dear Grandfather, I would really like my request to be answered as I would like to get out of debt, as I really don't deserve to be in this financial mess*. Something like that. What you are actually saying is dear grandfather I don't think I am worthy to get the help I am looking for. Why? Because you are asking for more of what you don't want. Remember the mind doesn't work in logic, only in what is plausible. Also, thoughts matter, what we think about brings energy and energy brings matter. If you are concentrating too much on what you don't want, you are going to bring more of what you don't want to you. Also coupled to this, we go moaning to our friends and family about what is missing from your life, and guess what? It is like you are advertising that fact to the world that you want more of the same. What needs to happen is to ask for that thing you do want and believe it is coming to you, don't even think about what you are lacking.

As thoughts bring matter, attract that thing you want by asking for it, but don't let the reason why you want it to come into your mind. The universe doesn't discriminate nor does it question what you are asking for, it simply obeys your request. However, we confuse the process by saying something like: *I would like a new job that pays better than what I have now, because I am struggling to cope with what I am earning.* That says I want more money and I also like to struggle. All you need to say is: *I thank you for my new well-paid position.* The universe knows what you earn, yes, believe it or not it does. That simple statement and the belief that you deserve and will get a new job that pays well, is being manifested for you. Makes sense? In other words, ask for what you desire, don't confuse the matter by stating why you want it, or maybe the reason why you won't get it. Just state what you want, feel it and see it coming to you, then let it go. Metaphysics also understands this, we bring to us what we believe. Example, when you were growing up you were told that if you went outside while it was raining and you got wet the chances would be you may catch a cold. I remember being told that when I was very young and it stayed with me for years. The truth is, it does not, a cold is simply a virus which can be caught at any time. But, as we were told that if I went out in the rain and got wet, or got cold on a winter day, and the following morning I awoke with a sneeze, I would say, "Yup, got a cold coming." Doesn't matter if it was genuinely just a sneeze, I would say to myself I have a cold coming. And as emotions and thoughts matter, we say I want a cold please. Now science would say 'ah, yes' but the cold virus lives in a body that has a temperature lower than bla bla bla! As that can be scientifically proven.

    I get that; however, as a virus is matter and we proclaim that we may have a cold coming, we invite that virus into our being. In my first book, I told of a lady that seemed to have brought cancer on at a certain age so that she could beat it and then carry on with her life. She foretold when the cancer would come and almost told the doctors when it would leave. She was spot on in both cases, scary thought, eh? What you believe and what you ask for is the magnet that attracts illnesses in your direction, your attitude and your positive and negative thoughts will determine that outcome for you, always, it is how the universal law works. You see if we use our minds to believe what we want or don't want, it responds, it is what the universe does, so the mind and the universe work as one. You see the mind stores all sorts of things from our experiences, what we believe, our opinions, principles and much more. It is these thoughts that will manifest within us to bring about physical issues like illness and pain and the mental problem the likes of anger, disharmony, stress and fear to name but a few. These, let's call them mind stores, are the driving factors of our physical and mental health. In modern society it is sometimes difficult not to feel things like stress, pressure and fear, after all the media does a great job of letting us know what's bad in the world. The mind responds tells the brain and that's when discord sets in. We have covered this, but as you see from a thought point of view, **we are what we think**. Remember, we are vibrational beings and connected to everything we see, hear, touch, taste and smell. We send negative vibrational messages through the mind or brain, which is also vibrating, it then sends messages to everything around us that we are happy or sad, positive or negative and our bodies react accordingly. We are perfect beings, no matter what physical issues we have, our higher selves, our subconscious is a perfect being. It cannot become ill, it does not sleep, it doesn't die has no fear and is infinite. It is an interesting thought, as that means whatever is affecting us in this world right now right here at this time, is simply down to your beliefs which you are allowing to manifest to the outside world. Wonder why we do that? When everything within us, within our higher selves, is calm and perfectly balanced. Perhaps knowing that will help us stay calmer when faced with a situation in life.

One thing to point out here is that you are totally different and unique to the next person. One person reading this will get a different idea of the text to the next. Your experience of something happy or sad, will be different to the next person. You have a different DNA to every other living thing on this planet, you are here to fulfil a destiny that no one else can achieve in this lifetime. We must take the time to take away the mask that we wear and become true to ourselves.

To do that we must also remove the negativity from our daily routines. I bet you are saying, yea right on the whole I am a positive person. Really? So exercise time, tomorrow just take the time to listen to yourself, be honest and if you can take a little notebook to make notes. I bet within a very short time after waking you have had at least four or five negative thoughts. Things like: *Got to leave early for work as the traffic is terrible, Ah, the kids! Why cannot they tidy up after themselves?* Or *I struggle to trust anyone these days, How much longer are they going to be in the bathroom?* Maybe *I cannot eat that it upsets me Oh! You didn't hear this from me, but!* or *I won't try that as I am terrible at it.* All these are general I know but do that exercise and smile when you realise that most days, we fill our day with negative thoughts. With these daily negative thoughts come that negative vibrational energy that will eventually grind down your body and mind.

Once you realise that, try to balance these thoughts to include a positive. Let me show you an example: *I won't try that as I am terrible at that, but maybe let me look on the internet or ask an expert and get some advice, at least then I can say I tried. Ah the kids, why can they not tidy up after themselves? So when they get home later, I will get them to put their things away by quietly explaining that we are all busy, but some help would be appreciated.* If you balance a negative with a positive outlook to that statement, you are taking the sting out of the negative and replacing it with a positive, and we know the body and mind will always respond to what we are telling it. Give something a positive outlook and we will respond in a positive way. I will give you another tip here, when in company, be it business or pleasure, don't respond to a negative comment or by the negativity of people's body language. You know you do it all the time, as the unconscious will have already picked up on it, and without you knowing it, it is sending you signals that you don't like that person. When you feel these thoughts and emotions come into your mind, just stop for a few seconds and realise that you do not have to agree to anyone for what they are. All you need to do is accept them for who they are, and that is a human being acting in a way that for them at that moment, at that time, is what they feel they need to do. Probably, and I am speaking generally here and from experience, I would say 90% of those people are not comfortable in a social gathering, they are acting in a way that counteracts the fear or uneasy feelings they are having at that time. The brash, party animal and the 'quiet sit in the corner person', are one in the same. They just disguise their fear and 'out of their comfort zone' feelings and thoughts by either being 'out there' or by being quiet 'in here'. They just try to disguise their fear in different ways. When in a social gathering, or even on the train or other public places, just realise certain people are not at ease and are just doing their best to disguise this uneasiness the best way they can. Is it an attack on you? No, (unless you have done something to harm a person either by physical or mental ways, if the answer to that is no), then take people at face value. Next time you feel you are surrounded by people who behave in an unlikely way, replace that 'idiot' thought, with 'okay they may be feeling nervous or fearful', so put their mind at ease, by being you. In a social gathering there will always be people acting out of character, by just being you, they may find that island of normality which family, social or work gatherings can sometimes knock out of us and we feel out of depth. Being that island will allow people to feel calm and centred around you. Don't be fooled and do not allow them to take you for granted, you are there as a friendly island of peace and are not there to be exploited. When in these social groups and you see these people out of character, just say to yourself: *I do not accept their behaviour I just accept them for who they are*. And unless you have a real issue with that person this will immediately calm your thoughts and behaviour to a positive nonaggressive one. Try it, but don't take my word for it get out there and give it a go, it really does work. This is a large subject and worthy of a book of its own, perhaps my third boo?

Before we move on let me just cover faith for you, as I think people use this 'faith' in the wrong way. Faith actually means a 'belief in the doctrines of a religion based on spiritual conviction rather than proof'. Kind of interesting don't you think? It states that people have faith in something where they don't actually have proof that it exists. When people tell me, "I have faith in that thing working," what you are actually stating is that you don't actually have an awareness that it will work, but you will try and see. All through the years, people say I have faith, but do they? Or is faith another word for hope? "I have hope in that thing working." Hope is another word for feeling an expectation and a desire for a particular thing to happen. Faith is something you think may happen but you don't have any proof it will, or does, and are perhaps hoping that it does or will happen, or not being the case. Not very convincing, is it? When people ask me about what I have faith in, I answer that I don't have faith in anything, however, I have a belief in a certain something. A belief is an acceptance that something exists or is true, to me. In other words, I have a knowing that, that thing, whatever it is, exists, or is going to work, or is in fact not going to work. Why am I going over this? As we believe in the words we use at a conscious level, we believe what we are saying to ourselves, and to others we speak to. An example, someone may ask, do I have faith in a particular project working. I will answer, "No, I have a belief in that project working." The difference? One is, I hope and think it may work but I am not 100% sure. The other is I have a trust in it working, because there is no reason for it failing. How can we break this down even further? Faith is something we wish for, it's almost like saying I **hope** it comes to me, where as a belief is stating that I **know** something will come to me. What we wish for comes to us, as we have seen and read above. When asking for something, remember use the correct words and consciousness will respect that thing you have asked for. When using words like may, might and could, you are using words that have potentially attached to them, they will keep the mind open and looking for possibilities. For example, if I am starting that project and say, "Yes, I **may** do it that way, or I **could** try it this way," those words are looking for possibilities. If you said, "I will do it that way," and it doesn't work, you have closed yourself and mind to looking for possibilities. When you say it could work that way, you are keeping your mind open and fluid, add belief and you are creating a powerful sense, let's have a look. **'I have a belief in the project working as we could do it that way.'** You are saying you have a knowing that it will work, however, putting in a 'could' keeps the mind open for any changes needed to keep that project on track. Now let's look at the other way if you say this, "I have faith in it working if we do it that way." Can you see the subtle difference? One is a possibility, the other a direct path. One is fluid, the other is a dead statement. One keeps the possibilities the other is saying it has to be done this way no matter what. All that does is close down all possible outcomes to one that fits what needs to be done. That's not how the universe works, it works in possibilities and will bring what you ask for as long as you have that belief in what you are asking for will come. Not necessarily in the way you want it to materialise, but it will come. Always remember, be careful what you ask for as if you ask it in the right way, that thing will come, it's the words we use that makes the statement of what we want more powerful.

As we are on the subject of thought and imagination, let's just cover off what fear is, as this is also important part of this chapter, as if we fear something, we may bring more of what we fear to us. Let's take a quick look at fear, then we can understand why we may ask for something in fear.

Basically, the fear emotion enters our lives, when we move into unfamiliar territory. Now this could be mental or a physical situation. In essence, it's that something that moves us out of our comfort zone. This feeling can stop us from moving forward in our lives, we may panic or find a way to move away from that situation, and then we resettle back on the same path or our comfort zone and life carries on as before. Fear is only a thought or a memory, but that thought or memory stays with us and as our conscious is constantly trying to take us away from pain and move us toward pleasure;

every time we come up against a certain situation, our minds remind us of that memory and we begin to panic and become fearful. Fear is only false evidence that manifests in a way that feels real. It doesn't really exist, only in that part of the mind that says it does. In any given situation, remember there is always a way out, if you can step back and look at that situation for what it is. If you can practice this, then you can understand where that fear comes from, then you can move from a fearful situation, into a situation that benefits you. In other words, don't concentrate on the negativity of that issue or problem, try and always look at the possible outcomes, those outcomes that you will benefit or understand. It could be that you just walk away, which in some circumstances is the best way. As my dear dad used to say, "Let's fall back and regroup," when things were getting a little out of our control. It's okay to fall back and see the bigger picture and then find a way to move forward. Take responsibility and don't blame those around you for your feelings, hurts and misfortunes. Only you create those feelings in your mind and unless you start to control those feelings, then you will have those trying times in your life. Times when you blame outside forces for these inner feelings, all you do at these times is give away all that personal power, which may result in having depression, pain and anxiety. The above was from my first book but also fits in here. Fear doesn't exist, it only manifests when you have negativity over certain thoughts. Your imagination is great at giving you a negative scenario about something you are about to do. Why give into something that may or may not happen? Don't allow negative thoughts to cloud your mind about something you want, ask for it with conviction with a belief that it will come to you. If you can replace a negative thought or image with a positive one, (as the void left from a negative thought has to be replaced) this will go a long way from a conscious point of view to building a strong positive mental image of that desire.

Remember you can trick your mind as the mind doesn't know what is real or imagined, it will just respond in either way. By replacing a negative with a positive, the mind will start to work on that and bring about the good feelings associated with that image. As there are no coincidences in the universe, the act of thought is pure energy. Remember we covered earlier in the book that 'thought = energy' and 'energy = matter'. Be positive about what you think about and replace a negative thought or feeling with a positive one and the conscious mind will assist. It is also important to remember that at times we need the negative to remind us that the positive exits, how? Simply that if you have a negative thought about something then that is a good thing, as it proves that we are giving thought to a particular thing, issue or whatever it is. If we can give something a negative thought, then we can also give that thing a positive thought by changing our perceptions about whatever it is we have that negative thought about. Negativity only exists in the part of us that says it does, in other words, breach that negative thought or fear as it may be using past experiences. This moment about to happen, has never happened before nor will it ever happen again. Don't let your conscious sabotage you, instead make it work for the positive good. Why do these negative thoughts pop into our mind in the first place? It's a survival thing, in the fact that when confronted by something new the unconscious will react in finding something from the past in order to match a behaviour to bring into play with this new situation. All it is doing is helping you by trying to keep you away from pain by reminding you of a situation that happened in the past. This is also brought into being when remembering something pleasurable that is about to happen, by reminding you of a similar past experience that you enjoyed. Let's face it, we won't get flustered by something pleasurable, it is those negative thoughts of fear from a past experience we don't like and try to run or hide from them. As we have just covered, don't run or hide from them see them for what they are and replace them by stating to yourself that:

"This is a new situation and although my conscious is reminding me of a past issue which was similar, this is in fact a new situation that has never happened before nor

will it happen again in this way again, therefore I shall stay in the moment and allow the power and grace of the universe to guide me in the direction I need to go in for my own harmony."

Then let it go, don't think about it again. I have used this time and time again; it does work and works well if you allow it to. Don't keep looking for answers and asking why me? And why this or that? Most of the time we have brought this issue to us by the way we think. If we can think that situation or issue into our lives, then we can think it out of our lives by using the information in this chapter to help you understand the basis of what we are and how thought and imagination plays such an important part in how we behave as a human.

Someone said to me once, 'Yes, I get this about the imagination and being the creative force in my life and how it turns out. But I am just one person; how can I change the world around me and really make a difference?' The answer is that you can, you are never one person, remember we are connected to everyone and everything around us. You making a positive change will create that ripple through the quantum energy soup and start to make things change and move in a positive way for the good of you and those around you. I am sure you can imagine a still pond, what happens when you throw a pebble into the water? It creates ripples, those ripples then flow out getting wider and wider until the water becomes still again. Here is a thought, those ripples that got wider and wider only stopped because the riverbank was there. If the bank wasn't there, those ripples would carry on getting wider and wider and bigger and bigger, they wouldn't stop, and why would they? There is nothing to stop them. As they get bigger, they become more powerful and if they become more powerful then they create more energy and thus brining that thing you desire into your existence. All we need is patience and more importantly, belief that the more powerful our ripples become the more energy they create, and then the more matter they will bring into our existence. In the above example of how a thought travels through time and space, our limited imaginations and lack of beliefs are represented by the riverbank. We create our ripples with a desire of what we want but then our lack of imaginations, beliefs and other factors limit those ripples until we create that bank to stop them from travelling further and becoming our desires. Don't create banks by limiting what you think will happen, think big don't set limitations and certainly don't stop believing in your desires, as in doing so will bring those banks to stop your ripples (desires) from traveling on and becoming bigger and more powerful.

When sending out your wishes or desires into the universe, remember that they will materialise but maybe not in the way you think they will. This life now, on this earth plane is a journey not a destination, this is a classroom and there are things we need to learn along our journey. This is natural and part of our existence, things will happen as we walk our path, but these are learnings we need to take on board, that's all, just learnings and challenges to be experienced. As long as we see issues and problems that may arise on our life's path as just learnings to be worked through, there will always be a positive outcome. In my first book I call these issues and challenges a 'tiger'. I will recap here:

I once had a very interesting chat with a Chinese Buddhist monk, wonderful man, full of sense and calm. I asked him, why in life we have challenges that sometimes I find it difficult to find a way around them as they arise. He said, "Why are you trying to find a way around them. You should embrace them."

I said, "Why should I embrace challenges; life is hard enough."

"But, without challenges," he said, "You cannot have growth, you cannot truly be the person you are meant to be." And as I like to put something tangible to explain things, I call life challenges 'a tiger' i.e. something I wasn't expecting to find on my journey. But something I can work through, understand, grow from and walk on. As my monk friend states, "We only get these challenges when the universe knows we are

ready to deal with it." The point is to understand what the challenge is, and why it arrived at that particular time of our lives, then work on a way around it, as at that time we will have all the answers we need, if we stop, listen and understand the learning that the 'tiger' represents at that time.

Don't let these 'tigers' detract you from your end goal, they are just a part of life's journey, they are just a natural part of our existence. These tigers won't cause the riverbanks to appear or stifle your wishes from expanding. In fact, they may cause your wishes to get stronger as you are understanding and dealing with these challenges or banks as they appear, thus eliminating them from your end goal. Challenges are there to help us see the bigger picture, at times sure they will take us out of our comfort zone, but that's okay, as getting out of our comfort zone is all part of growth. I have a theory that has been tried and tested. If you take those challenges and allow yourself to move out of your comfort zone now and again, then life, or the universe, will help you along your path. It's those times when we procrastinate that life will sometimes give us a kick in order to help us along the way. You know those times when something happens that really takes us out of our comfort zone with that 'Oh, I really wasn't expecting that' or 'I really didn't deserve that' attitude. Take time each day to move out of your comfort zone, it doesn't need to be anything drastic, just a little change to your routine is sometimes all that is needed. A little deviation from the main topic of this chapter, however, I thought at this stage it was important to put this in.

I think at this point before we close this chapter, which as mentioned could be a book in itself, let's recap on the main points as I wanted this to be a taster for you to discover more about the amazing world of metaphysics. Which when looked at, bolts on nicely to what quantum mechanics and what this book is trying to do, which is as always, open your mind to a world of possibilities.

In this chapter we have seen that the mind controls who we believe we are, but with imagination you can take back that control. As the mind doesn't know what is real or imaginary, we can trick it into believing what we want it to believe. Trouble is these days, we don't take control, we let the mind dictate to us or push us onto a path we don't necessarily want to go down, and sometimes we don't realise this until it's too late. Start taking back control, it is easy once you understand that by letting the imagination go, it can bring you the life you desire and if you believe it is yours it will be. The body and the universe will follow, remember the equation which is thoughts = energy = matter. That thing that you put your thoughts to will manifest its energy, it has to it's how the universe works. Once the energy is engaged it will bring matter, or that thing you thought about, be it positive or negative. If it is a negative then this can also be a positive, why? Because negatives bring positives by simply reminding you that you are obviously thinking about that thing you don't want, not the thing you do want. We also covered that the mind only works in what's plausible, think about the think you don't want and it will appear, as the mind has to think about something in order not to think about it, thus brining that thing to you. Thoughts bring energy which brings matter. Program your mind into bringing forth that thing you do want, don't start thinking about what you don't want. If you want a new job think about all the positives that new job will bring. If you start to think about the reason you don't like your present job, then more of that negative will flow into your life. Remember to think about that thing you do want. Then you create the ripples that will flow out from your thoughts and get stronger and stronger. Don't create those riverbanks by putting in restrictions, allow those ripples (desires) to flow out into the universe and get bigger and stronger by allowing them the freedom to create, by simply keeping positive with a belief that the thing you want will come to you. Problem in society these days is children and in fact adults are not allowed to use their imagination by all this new technology that is flooding into our everyday existence. Ah! I hear you shout, this is needed to keep up with the modern world. Perhaps it is, but without the great people of the past like Aristotle, Einstein,

James Watt and Leonardo De Vinci using their imaginations, we wouldn't be here where we are now. They didn't use a computer program or tablet or mobile phone, they simply allowed their imaginations to shine through. I will leave you with that thought, as I hope it may make you realise that if we allow a little imagination into our everyday lives, it can only open our minds to think beyond the limits of what we think is possible.

Chapter Thirteen
Senses

Having explored our imagination and thoughts it may be a good time to cover our senses, as understanding these may also help us to further understand the world around us. What are our basic senses we use every day? Well, those would be classed under the nervous sensory system the five important ones are what we use to see, hear, touch, taste and smell. These are the basic recognised senses we all have and share and are all connected to the Parietal lobe of the brain. This part of the brain lets us know what is part of the body and what is part of the outside world. The parietal lobe is connected to the cerebrum, and not to go into too much depth here, but the cerebrum in humans is a large part of the brain and is the uppermost region of the central nervous system. I won't go into detail between the differences of the five senses as they really speak for themselves. So, to just cover them off (actually there are other sense's two of which are the proprioception which is the perception of the body position at any given time and is important for balance in movement, and thought, which we covered earlier), we will briefly look at them here.

See: *Is what we engage through the eyes, which detects colour and light. The light enters the eye then moves through the pupil and then onto the retina to the receptors in the brain through the option nerve. The brain interprets this information and then makes sense of what we are seeing. Funny, isn't it?, that it's not the eyes making sense of what we are* *seeing, they are, in all intense and purposes, just the receiver of light which is passed back into the brain for processing.*

Hear: *This sense manifests through the ears. The vibrations then extend to the inner ear through special bones called the hammer, anvil and stirrup which in turn pass the information it has gained into the brain. The brain then advises on the information it has gained and lets us know what noise it is we have just heard.*

Touch: *Touch comes through the skin and detects what we are physically touching be it cold, hot, hard, sticky or pain etc. The skin has many nerve receptors that sense the level of pressure being applied at that time. The information is sent via the peripheral nervous system to the central nervous system and into the brain. The brain again interprets this information and advises on what we are touching at that given moment.*

Taste: *This is manifested through the tongue which detects the different tastes it is being presented with. This could be bitter, sour, sweet in fact the list is huge. The taste buds on the tongue, which are the sensory organs, are responsible for distinguishing between substances that we find pleasing as well as those which are not so pleasurable. The taste buds could also alert us to things that maybe harmful like poisons.*

Smell: *Smell manifests through the nose, which picks up scents from the air. These smells are then directed straight into the olfactory cortex of the brain. This then breaks down the information into a particular smell and lets us know whether we like it or not.*

That gives you a basic break down of the five main senses we use to make sense (no pun intended) of the world around us. Nothing too complicated there and nothing new from that which you probably already know. Here comes the science bit, and I love this part. All the above takes on average one thousandth of a second to process whatever it is we are touching, tasting, smelling, hearing or indeed seeing, in affect everything thing we use to navigate our world from a physical point of view is always in the past. Nothing is now, or here right now, it cannot be as if it takes a thousandth of a second to work out what it is, we are actually sensing, then the time the brain works it out and sends that information back to us, it is doing so in the past tense. It is giving us the information we need from whatever it is we are sensing after the event has happened. Nothing is now, every bit of information we receive is for something that has already happened and in the past. Yes, okay, one thousandth of a second is a very, very quick period of time, but the fact remains that if it takes that time to process information on something that is happening right now and that information comes to us after the event, then that event it relates to, is already gone and it's in the past. Interesting thought isn't it? In essence, we shouldn't be worrying about anything as everything we sense in our physical lives has already gone and is not existing at this time. Thought it would be good to share that with you as it got me thinking about all sorts of things. Yes, I know I need to get out more!

Moving on, we all have these five basis senses, apart from the obvious issues with being blind or deaf, to which these people miss out on life's sights and sounds. In theory most of us have these five senses. Another thing to point out here is that although we all have the sense to listen and hear, we all use this information in a slightly different way to each other. One person will have the need to listen constantly to everything around them. They are the annoying ones that can have a constant barrage of background noise or music, yet at the same time have an incredible ability to concentrate on what they are doing. Another may use sight to make sense of their worlds and that saying 'seeing is believing' strikes true to them. I had an auntie who was just like that, on her birthday if I rang her on the phone to say happy birthday and that I loved her. She would say, "Oh that's nice," in a slightly condescending way. However, if I sent her flowers with a note to say happy birthday and I love you, she would believe me more. Why? Because she used her eyes, her sight to make sense of the world more than someone who likes having noise as a constant companion. She could understand more of her world by me sending something she could see and read, which made more sense to her than me stating that I loved her over the phone using just speak. She was in fact a visual person, making sense of what she saw was all important.

That gives you a brief idea of the physical senses, what they are and what they do. Now, there are others out there that say we have more than five senses and that we may have 10 or even 20. The five main senses we use to navigate our world are noted above, which, as I already stated, you probably know already.

The above is the physical, but as you all know, I also like to look at the spiritual. I am now going to take this opportunity to look at the famous sixth sense, that part of us that the movies have made to look mysterious and strange. Which in fact isn't strange or mysterious at all and is just another part of us that some have, or can tap into. The sixth sense is that part of us that goes beyond the traditional five senses we covered earlier. It is that part that mediums or psychics use to communicate with the energies of others that have passed, or indeed are still alive. I use this when I communicate with people or indeed animals that have moved on from this life. Okay, I hear you groan and say that there is no proof of this, but if you recall from the previous chapters, there is in fact, more proof than you realise. Science is forever making inroads in discovering that there is a life after death due to the way energy simply changes its form when we leave our physical bodies. Being a medium means I can speak to the ones passed away by tapping into their energy. Medium for me is a strange word as it implies something witchy or wizard, but this ability is open to everyone if we take time to practice and open to it. If you read back through the previous chapters, you may remember we are all spiritual energy having a human experience. This sixth sense is just a way that some people use to communicate with others. It is still a sense we have, just some are more attuned to it than others but my belief is that we all have the ability to do this, if we choose. That's it, nothing complicated or mysterious, the sixth sense is just a part of who we are it is just us, all of us, that allows us to be aware of a higher presence and energy that is not a part of our physical being. We can sometimes sense this sixthness (just invented that, sixthness) when we are in that twilight zone just before sleeping when we feel ourselves drift away from our physical selves. We get that light floating feeling; our minds seem to drift off to a more enlightened almost parallel place where we feel a calmness and a sense of detachment from the physical. This feeling is the opening to the higher plane where we all end up. When I help people tap into this realm to speak to loved ones who have passed, I always get that sense of calm and detachment from the physical it is so nice, it's sometimes hard to come back to the here and now. The sixth sense is that natural part of us that opens the doors, so to speak, to that higher energy field of awareness.

I hope that makes sense and you understand that we have a sixth sense, which isn't attuned to just being a Hollywood film. If we take the time, we may realise that we have these six senses and that apart from the basics we use, what we hear, see, touch, taste and smell there is the sixth sense and also a seventh. If the sixth sense is the spiritual opening that allows us to be able to tap into that higher energy, we all possess from that unconscious level, then what's the seventh? Well, that is an interesting question. The seventh sense is that ability to move into the doorway of consciousness where we can access a sense of being beyond the physical being. This doorway opens the consciousness to information and learnings almost like a library situated at the centre of the universe. Sounds like something from Harry Potter, doesn't it? Or from a Star Wars film. But there is a place called the Akashic Records and is available to everyone. Ah, I hear you say 'more mystic rubbish!' Or is it? Where do you think the answers come from when you ask a question on a topic or even a deeper question about life, when after a period of time the answer suddenly pops into your head. Or you see the answer you are looking for in the street or on an advert, etc. It comes to you from this

Akashic records where everything is stored. All you need to do is ask the question, forget about it and the answer will come, you don't need to search for it; have patience and it will be revealed to you. The seventh sense is the ability to understand that this information is there by allowing yourself the luxury of entering this doorway of a deeper spiritual consciousness. This consciousness allows you a perception of using information from a higher place. The perception of not only asking questions about all sorts of physical and spiritual questions, but by also guiding you to everyday experiences. Have you ever walked into a place and immediately felt you were in familiar surroundings without actually having been there before? Then that is your seventh sense at work. We have all had that Deja Vu moment where we feel at a present moment in time, we have had the notion we have either been there before, or we feel we have experienced that situation at another occasion. That again is your seventh sense at work. How does this particular sense work? It's at those times when you unconsciously, and sometimes consciously, bring forward to you all the resources and information to you from everything around you, including our friend that quantum energy soup. At this time, all become transparent and nothing is hidden, you open yourself to creation and the three parts of past, present and the future all merge together. During these times when you open completely to everything around you, you are letting all that spiritual energy and information to come into your existence, and at most times we do this without even knowing. It is those times we get those notions of knowing the answer to anything, you feel empowered, enriched, energised with a sense of calm and belonging. Not a bad place to be, eh? When you feel empowered and at a higher self, you suddenly realise that you are not a part of this physical plane, you are just passing through. Perhaps then you know that you are from somewhere much higher and of a pure, intelligent and knowing place which you have forgotten while you are here, but a place you will return once your leanings of this world has been finished. Some of this has been proven where studies in quantum physics has discovered the zero-point theory. This is a sea of energy that is invisible but is constant throughout the universe. This energy moves in waves and is known as quantum waves and the way to engage with the seventh sense is to connect to these quantum waves. Everyone being on the planet has the ability to tap into these waves of information that some call the Akashic records. This is not some idea that certain people have it is a fact and has been proven by science by the likes of Richard Feynman. He discovered that the electrical impulses in our brains can be activated by these quantum waves, by subatomic particles being able to pass on information from any given distance and simultaneously. We won't go too deep into that, as that is better explained by people like Richard and another quantum physicist. But basically, what happens is that the electrons in our brains create radiation, that makes us capable of receiving radio waves of information from the past. Which also means, that due to the balance needed in nature we can receive radio signals from the future. This information can be transmitted through the universe instantly at any time. Sounds a bit far-fetched, doesn't it? Imagine if you will, that we can access this library or Akashic records at any time to gain information, which is something we may forget if we rely too much on artificial intelligence giving us the information we require. I believe the ancients knew how to tap into this information like the Mayans and the Egyptians etc. As mentioned earlier, we forgot how to use this basic of functionality we at liberty to use. By the way, this isn't a new thing, people like Einstein and as far back as 1883 when this idea was made public by the author Alfred Percy Sinnett; who describes that Eastern philosophy know that universal records exist through what they call Akasa, which means ether, which is now what we call Akashic. People of the past knew of these records and ideas and now science is catching on. It always amazes me that the peoples of the past knew all about these mystical references and now they are being discovered by science. What did the ancients do that we don't do now? They used their sixth and seventh senses to make sense of and understand their world. Are there any more senses we should be aware of?

Some research suggests you could have as many as 20 senses. I am not 100% sure about that, if everything you need to learn comes from the learning you have here on this earth which are the five senses, and we have that knowing of the sixth and seventh senses, then I think that anymore may start to become confusing and unnecessary. Remember things in nature are not complicated and that goes for us too, so why have more than the basics to help us navigate through this life and make us realise we are also connected to something much higher.

As you can see, the first five senses are the physical but the higher the number, the more spiritual we become. The sixth sense is the psychic level, letting us become aware of the energy round us and of that around others. The seventh sense is the higher inner you, that part of you that lives within the physical body. Do we need all seven to help us navigate this life of the here and now, I would say yes for sure we do and perhaps it's because we have lost the ability to use the sixth and seventh senses that we struggle at times with the physical. As I am sure you have sensed that there is more to you than what we just hear, see, taste, touch and smell. There has to be, as otherwise just those senses alone wouldn't cause us to have those times when we stand back and ask ourselves that there must be more to us than just tracking through the physical. After all, if we just used those five senses then who is doing the observing of the physical you, or maybe a higher spiritual you? I will leave this chapter here, it was just to make you realise that we have more than just what we use on a day-to-day basis to work with. Take time to contemplate this chapter as it may get you to ask more questions, which is what this short chapter was designed to do.

Conclusion

This part of the book was about allowing your mind to expand and ask questions, as I believe if we ask questions then we learn, if we chose not to ask questions and take the everyday as all there is, then we simply exist. The idea for the '*Human Whisperer'* was to get you to open up to new ideas and theories that were or are in your periphery. This book could be a manual that may open your understanding a bit more about the world around you.

We have looked at what a whisperer is, we explored what your psyche is and asked you to realise that your thoughts carry energy and that this energy can have an effect on not only things around you, but also those around you. We looked at nature and how nature is an important part of us, we cannot just go through life ignoring that aspect that allows us to survive as a race of people. We are a part of nature, so take time to stand back and appreciate her for what she is and what she is teaching us. We covered what the meaning of life may be and asked you to look at it in another dimension, thus allowing you to see your life in this world. Next we looked at the birth of consciousness and the confusion that science and history still have around this important part of who we are. I think that once we crack that then it will bring a new awareness to what a human being really is. It will then flow into 'who am I', 'what am I capable of' and 'what resources do I have around me to help me grow at this time on earth'. It may open you to new learnings as you realise you are more than you thought you were. The old tradition of the Shaman which has been practiced for many thousands of years, may make you realise that although we are moving forward with technology, we also have to understand our past and through these old practices we can still tap into that old knowledge that will keep us on the spiritual path to understanding us and the world around us. If we can do that, then we can remember that imagination and thoughts, due the fact they also bring energy, can bring about our desires. As, keep in mind, thoughts bring energy and energy brings matter it is that simple. Practice this and understand it, it will bring those changes in your life. Finally, understand that we have our senses, those that guide us through the physical life and those that tap into or coincide with our spiritual existence. We as people spend much too much time living with the five basics of what we hear, touch, taste, see and smell. Open your being to the two spiritual ones the sixth and seventh senses then combine them with the five physical ones. You may be surprised at how the world suddenly opens up to all sorts of wonderful experiences.

I hope you found this part of the book thought provoking and giving you a sense that there is so much more around us if we take the time to tap into this amazing spiritual path we are on. It's always been a part of us, but we have lost our way a little due to advancements in things like technology that takes away the ability to think for ourselves and use common sense. The second part of this book is going to look at the '*The Last Spark*', there is a saying when people have an idea or when someone says something intelligent, people say, "Oh, look at you, you bright spark." The next part I am going to look at is what may be the last spark, as we throw away some of what we need to continue to strive on this planet.

The Last Spark

This part of the book was going to be a chapter, but as I think it's important to get this message across it will be a section within the book. What has it got to do with being a human whisperer? Well, everything and nothing to be honest, why? Because I feel there is more confusion and mistrust around now, than probably at any time in human evolution, so I thought it would be good to put this in, as without a deeper realisation as to where we are heading and to what may be happening, getting you to understand more about you and the world around you will be futile. So, welcome to this part of the book '*The Last Spark*'. What is the last spark? Well, I hope it will induce the 'spark' of an understanding within your deeper being that unless we start to take on board the realisation that you are a part of nature and nature a part of you, as we covered in the first part of this book, and that unless we really start to get a grip with what may be changing to our world then we will struggle in the years to come. There are a lot of prophecies around at the moment all stating that we are entering, or have entered a fifth dimension, or that the earth has tilted on its axis, as it seems to do every twenty-six thousand years. Could any of these be right? Possibly, but you know there is a simpler explanation and one that I feel resonates with us all. We, us, humans have caused these modern issues for ourselves. I feel we have lost the ability to be creative, use our imagination and common sense, we have also bitten the hand that feeds us, i.e. nature. Is this part of the book going to be hard hitting? Yes, it will also be creative and objective; it will get you to use your imagination and stand back and look at what we are doing to ourselves, which will and does have an effect on our planet. It will look at the spiritual, the conscious, subconscious and above all, it will hopefully get you to engage with good old-fashioned common sense to change perceptions of who we are before it really does become too late.

I feel and I know I am not alone in this, that people, the world and nature are becoming confused and not following a set pattern as it used to. People seem far too angry, upset, annoyed and just set for looking out for themselves, rather than the collective good like we used to be. Nature has become unsettled with varying weather patterns we have not seen before. If you take time to connect to nature, which I know 90% of us don't, then you will feel an imbalance with all things. There is a reluctance for change, it is almost like nature is being pulled in a way it isn't used to, and like us, it's a little confusing and unyielding. In trying to retain that balance, things have become a little puzzling and out of kilter. You may think I am talking rubbish, but take a moment, to look around you. If you are old enough, look back to 40 or 50 years ago, remember what was different. People were happier, weather systems were more stable and nature was in abundance. I am not talking about the difference between hot summers of 1976 and 2018. But I am talking about a balance that nature and the weather brought. It stabilised us as humans, we knew where we were with things, we understood more about the nature around us, even if we didn't think we did. We took time to go out in it, enjoy it, go for walks with the children and climb trees. We took the time to connect even if we didn't know that at a conscious level. When I look back at my time growing up, I was hardly in the house, I was always out playing somewhere, coming back for lunch or dinner then going out again. If my father's car was playing up, he would go out open the bonnet and fix it. If something in the house needed work doing to it, we would do whatever it was which was needed. We grew vegetables in the garden, it wasn't a large garden but we grew carrots and beans etc. we also found the time to go out and enjoy nature and understand what she brought to us. Music in the charts was so unique, in the top 10 records in those times you had such an eclectic mix of music. We had disco, country and western, rock, punk and even some classical all in the top 10. Yea, okay! Kids reading this, may say, what are you talking about? We had a thing called diversity which isn't there these days.

I have an opinion of the present chart music, which funnily enough sounds like my father when I was young when he described the music I listen to. The point is, there aren't any variations in something as basic as records in a top 10 listening survey. We seem to follow a set pattern of what's in vogue at that time, there isn't a good variation of ideas and in the last example of music we seem to become more lemming like in following what everyone else follows. Different kinds of music are now driven away until it becomes in vogue again, when it may get a revival. Years ago, all different genres of music were allowed to be played at the same time, people got it and engaged with it. That was a generalised example, but the point is, we are becoming lemmings we don't seem to have that decision of choice that will allow so many different types of music to be played at the same time. The sad fact of the matter is that I don't think it will be the same again unless we change our attitude to having that ability to make choices. Society at this moment doesn't like people to have individual choices, it tends to put people in set groups, as it likes to make people easier to understand by others. I get that to a certain point, why complicate things by giving us too many choices. At the same time without choices we become followers of others, it is like someone has taken away that decision process from us. If that is allowed to happen, then what do we become? In fact it's more interesting to see what we do become and that is, lap dogs. We lose that ability to think for ourselves and use common sense; and why would we use these abilities when decisions are made for us? It may take a few generations but it is happening and that is why I feel we are becoming confused, angry and frustrated. What brought about this change? What brought on our inability to use our imaginations to become followers rather than being innovative, caring and spiritual toward others? I think the first basis is that we have forgotten that we have a higher self, that part of us that is unique to us and no-one else. It's like our physical DNA that is unique to you, it is different to everyone else, that makes you different to all seven billion people on this planet. That in itself must make you realise that you are special and that if you are different to everyone else, you have your own mind and capabilities, yet we fail to use this idea.

Remember, in Chapter 13 we talked about our senses and in particular the seventh sense, saying that the seventh sense is the doorway to perception and the higher self. Perhaps as humans we need to tap into this, perhaps this is the missing link to why we are becoming who we are. Going back to basics to understand this concept, will take us away from following others with a realisation that you are more than the flesh and bones that allows you to move around this planet. Technology is also a driver of taking away the ability to use common sense as it stops you from seeking out answers to your questions, as all you need to do is tap a few keys and get a complete response to whet ever it is you need. Some of this is a good thing but taking away your ability to use your mind and imaginations to work out an answer is not a good thing. All that does is make the mind lazy and as we read in a previous chapter, if we don't use certain neurons these will die off. In effect, causing our brains to become less useful and causing confusion and frustrations when confronted with a problem or issue we don't understand. If we are using technology and AI more and more, we are losing the ability to tap into this higher state of being. It's almost like we are becoming cavemen again in not having that frontal lobe ability to use common sense and to use the energy and spiritual learnings that are out there and within here that is buried within us. We become lost in the artificial leanings and as a result also lose the ability to use the imagination which is where the greatest ideas, inventions and concepts of the past have come from. Sure, technology makes us more comfortable but it also takes away our ability to think for ourselves, this is when that seventh sense should come into play. The less we use our spiritual sense, the less we become masters of our universal lives as we become dependent on others to make decisions for us. Let me make another comparison as I feel this is an important point to grasp. There has to be a balance to all things and as I mentioned earlier, I understand the need for technology. But if there is too much to one side, we become unbalanced and we capsize. If we are building our lives and we want to build a mountain, we dig a hole to move the earth from that hole to put it on top of other earth to build that mountain. Great, the mountain grows and gets bigger, however, at the same time we are creating a hole and as the mountain grows, the hole gets larger. The cause and effect of building our lives sometimes leaves an emptiness in other parts. With technology helping us to grow our lives, it sometimes forgets, as it's artificial, that while helping us grow it leaves voids in other parts of our lives. If we use AI too much, then we forget that there is that hole or void as we rush to become this bigger or better person. That hole I am talking about is common sense, that if we take, we have to give back, as one day you are walking around your life and guess what? Yes, you may fall down that hole you created. AI will and does help you grow and bring the world to your fingertips with regard to information and communication. Balance this with the good old-fashioned way of using your mind to create the world you desire by getting back to basics and working with you, your imaginations and getting out and understand the world around you. The balance has to be there as otherwise we will become followers and all fall into those holes we created. We understand that there is a positive and a negative. The negative, at times, needs to be there so we can understand the positive. In effect it's not really a negative it's just our perception of a problem or issue that manifests in a way that we see it as having a negative impact on our lives. Sometimes, it is just a sign showing us that maybe we are on the wrong path and need to change. These negatives create a balance with the positive, at times you cannot have one without the other. If we continue to build these mountains and we forget about the holes we create in making these mountains, then the imbalance forms and we forget, that these holes must be recognised as otherwise we will fall into them. That's where I feel AI leaves us, it gives us the realisation that we can better ourselves with technology. However, we forget about the other sides of the human psyche at our detriment, as if at a later stage we come across one of these holes we won't have a clue on how to deal with it. I hope that makes sense as in a nutshell, we rely too much on technology and forget about common sense and realising who we are. We then become the same as everyone else and when issues or problems crop up, we will lose that common-sense factor in knowing how to deal with these issues and problems. You can program AI to turn the lights on, make dinner clean and help us to drive from A to B while avoiding traffic. BUT you cannot program it to be human, no matter how intelligent it is, it won't be able to tap into the quantum energy/waves. That is where it will come undone and us too, if we don't keep the old ways going. We may become nurtured and universally ignorant forgetting that we are a part of nature and not a computer chip.

Here is a scary thought, one that I believe is already happening the day we cloned a sheep called Dolly in 1996. Have we, or are we entering a stage of human evolution where we can change the structure of us as a human being by modifying our DNA? We have discovered DNA and therefore we have in theory, read the book of life. If we have in fact done that, we know what needs to be done in order to change some illnesses and in time perhaps some life-threatening conditions. But, can changing our DNA also change our human qualities, make us calmer or indeed make us more aggressive? I believe we are more complex to change our characters completely, can science change some aspects of us as a human being? I believe the answer is yes, we grow genetically modified crops so why can we not make genetically modified human beings? Perhaps we already are when couples go for IVF treatment, who knows? Yes, okay, that sounds like a conspiracy theory, but why not? I have come across a lot of interesting facts while doing some research. Anyway, that's for another day and time. A further thought that if we are allowed or indeed, if these genetically modified humans start to walk the planet, they could have a much higher IQ then the rest of us, that could see us be ruled by 'artificial humans' capable of a higher intellect then the common man/woman. Scary concept? At the moment, there must be laws preventing this from happening, but if we lose the common sense ability to think for ourselves, perhaps if these beings came into our existence, then would we know? Our reliability on AI could get to a point where these 'new order humans' (let's call them), seem the normal to us. That is just a theory for you to ponder, but hence the reason why we really do need to keep the balance between using our brains and working with technology.

Anyhow, let's get back on track, but the above is a scary thought and one to ponder? Could it be true? Well, we will find out as the future rolls on. The future, that is an interesting subject and as we are covering this with what maybe the last spark, let's see if we can predict the future with where we are now. This could be an eye opener, so let's see where it takes us. As we read above, if we let too much AI into our world, we are switching off our ability to make the correct assumptions about us, our evolution and that can only be a bad thing. Let's look at some facts, the planet is becoming too small for us as we become overpopulated, natural resources have been drained at an alarming rate, deforestation, the ice caps are melting with rising temperatures caused by climate change, not to mention, the continued wars and issues of famine and a lack of water caused by climate change in certain points around the world. It also seems that people are becoming more fearful and uncertain about their individual lives. Why are people becoming like that? It's because nature has changed and is struggling and we, as we read in Chapter 2, are connected to nature, we can feel this uncertainty and change but we cannot work out how to help. To be honest, I don't think we can help. You see we have been talking about the effects of gasses, fossil fuels, waste and all manner of issues as long as I have been on this planet, which is close on 56 years and yet we have barely done anything about it. In fact, the rain forests are still being cut down at an alarming rate causing an imbalance of carbon dioxide in our atmospheres and what do we do? Oh yes, we have a world forum on the subject that is due to be held in another couple of years. Really, in a couple of years? At which time an area the size of Wales will have gone. Ah yes, I hear but we will re-plant. Excellent idea that will take at least another 30–60 years before the trees are efficient enough to replace the ones we cut down. Here is an idea, STOP cutting down the rainforest and instead look at alternatives to timber, come on people we are in the 21st century have we really lost the ability to use our imaginations to come up with another material to use instead of timber? Ah yes, probably not as AI hasn't come up with an alternative yet. Politicians like to think they are addressing these issues and some do take it seriously. However, I don't feel that the majority do as they fuss over the scraps of political power, instead of focusing on the real issues, as at some stage if we carry on like this there won't be any scraps left. Just a load of man-made crumbs that won't sustain anyone let alone a political prowess. Right now, I am sure that we are entering a stage that if we don't act immediately on these important issues then we won't know how to reverse the effects of our slow response to getting some of these issues corrected. If the likes of global warming are not reversed, then global warming may become self-sustaining and as the polar caps are melting then it reduces the amount of solar energy reflected back into space making the temperature increase within our planet. Not to mention the obvious which is the sea levels rising and causing floods and erosion to our planet making the land masses smaller, which is just what we want in an ever-increasing population. If that happens, we can count the number of years we have left before nature intervenes and takes back control. Another impact of our ever-increasing ignorance to the planet, did you know in the last century we have managed to kill of over 500 species? Most of this was caused by us and our greed to take more back from the earth and by doing so pushing some species to extinction. These include creatures like the Western Black Rhinoceros, the Monk Seal, The Pyrenean Ibex and the Japanese Sea lion. Then there are animals on the endangered list including the Gorillas, Sea Turtles, Orangutan, the Tiger, Sumatran Elephant and the Amur Leopard. All gone or about to go due to us, humans pushing them from existence by our greed to take. A generalised example here, I was on the train recently coming back from London. I was sharing the carriage unfortunately with two young yuppie types. There was a horrible harrowing picture in the paper of a humpbacked whale with a large piece of plastic stuck in its mouth that it was struggling to remove. These two, (let's be polite and call them gentleman), were laughing as one made a comment that at least this poor whale wouldn't need to floss anymore. Most of the people around these idiots looked in disgust at this stupid comment, to which they got some abuse of 'what are you looking at'? Before they went back to their sneers and then picked up their mobile phones and started messaging or whatever it was they were doing. If that is what the young well-dressed and well-educated kids think of our planet, then I don't give much hope for the future. We have to realise that if our planet is going the way it is, it will begin to falter as nature starts to take back control. One thought to consider, if this is allowed to happen then where will we go? Space isn't an option as we are yet to come even close to building another life for us on another planet. This is all we have people, wake up and realise that this is happening now. I am not being an environmentalist, although I understand where they are coming from. I am seeing this as a person being able to connect to the greater universe, the same as we all can. I am not unique there are lots of others like me, which are able to tap into nature and also being psychic means I can sense things at a higher level, something we can all do if we take time to understand it and open up our minds. The message I am picking up now is of a fearful world, where people are confused and worried. This is more on an unconscious level, but it is happening. If you don't believe me, ask around, ask your friends, family and work colleagues. Ask them to be honest, totally honest and see what their reaction is. Someone told me recently that if the human growth rate continues as it is now, in another two thousand years with all the electricity being generated, the planet would physically glow red. When I was at school many years ago now, we were asked by the teacher what would be the biggest threat to our planet. Most of us said an asteroid or being hit by some other space debris. She said no climate change, but governments are doing something about it, so as such yes it could be a meteor or some kind of space debris. Now 45 years on, she was right, it is climate change and yet in the 45 years since she asked us that question, not much has been done about it, and in fact, more has been done to escalate its rapid increase to a point that I am not sure how much time we have before nature steps in. And at that point, I don't want to be on this planet we call home, as when nature takes back control, it won't be a pretty sight.

What could the future be like? As we have seen the negative, as always there has to be a positive to any negative. I believe that we must first remember that we are spiritual beings having a human experience. Take time to connect with you/nature, and this can be a simple walk in the park or in the countryside somewhere. A place that you can be quiet and just take time to appreciate and listen to the sounds around you. Clear your mind from the modern-day clutter of work or the traffic, release anger and frustration and just be. Switch off and just enjoy that quiet time. You may feel a little more adventurous, so try some meditation or mindfulness. If you really want to change, then try going to a mediumship circle. Be wise and check these out first as there are a lot of well-meaning people that don't really have the knowledge or gift to teach. Any of the above will allow you time to clear your thoughts. Thoughts and the mind are like a muddy fish tank, if you keep stirring up the water it will become murky, or in our case the mind will be filled with all sorts of things. Leave the tank a few hours and the water will become clear as the mud settles. Just like our minds, leave it to settle by spending time in nature, or doing a nice meditation and the mind will become settled and clear. We also need to have a good imagination, but as we have already covered this several times already, we will leave that there. Just to say that without a good imagination we cannot move forward, as this is a fundamental part of who we are. This doesn't mean we just need an imagination to invent new things, we also need a good imagination to make the people that can make a change to our planet sit up and take notice. These points are important if we are to take charge of our planet and make the changes necessary for our survival. If we take the time to stand back and look at things for what they are, or for what they are becoming, we can start to make those all-important changes to our lives that will have a significant positive step forward for others. Do we want to be driven to a brainless quest for intelligence or do we want to take back control through a higher plane where we can see things as they go wrong and make subtle changes to our world that will enable its success and future? We are on the edge of causing untold damage to our home and this damage will cause us to suffer in the future. The two idiots I spoke about earlier on the train are the type of people that will keep taking and not realising the problems they are causing as they seek to build their future born of ignorance and fear. Why do I say they are fearful? Simply because the fuss and noise they make, it's not confidence it's just arrogance which comes from being afraid. The issue is they probably don't realise it and will continue to move through their lives running away from something. Those that stop and listen to what is happening from a higher consciousness point of view will and can make the difference. They engage with the universe and can sense and feel the hurt we are causing to not only the planet but to ourselves. I, at times, have a really foreboding feeling run through my body. When I find a quiet time, which I find fairy quickly after having these feelings, I tune into the frequency of nature. Now before you say, "Here we go, more hippy stuff," let me say that as mentioned we are all connected to each other and the planet through the quantum energy soup, that science has proven exists. So, I find time and engage with this energy and I can feel the pain and the hurt felt by nature and by thousands of people as we continue to ravage our home. I and many others feel this pain getting stronger and I believe if we keep moving down this destructive path, there will be a point where nature will take back control. That's why it is so important more people let go of modern life just for a few minutes, hours, a week – get out in nature and you will see the struggle. At the same time, you will also see the beauty and majesty of this wonderful planet. Perhaps that is the most important message, see the beauty and the majesty, feel the sun, see the wildlife and feel alive when out in fresh air. Then perhaps this may make you realise there is a gentle balance to all things and remember these wonderful good feelings and thoughts you get when outside. Then make up your mind to do your part in helping keep this planet a good place to be. It doesn't take much, remember, small steps make a big difference.

If we are to change, we need to learn and to keep learning, as this is the fundamental part of who we are. We are a learning machine we need to keep learning and absorbing information. At a subconscious level, we do this all the time by taking on around +17 million bits of information a second every second which is 500 thousand times more than the conscious mind works with on a second by second basis. We start learning when we are a baby and it basically continues until we pass. If that is the case and we are continually learning, then why don't we put what we are learning to good use? I believe it's because we think learning only takes place in a classroom or workshops at work etc. Truth is, we are learning as we go about our lives, it involves the whole person what we gather from our five senses, but also our beliefs about who we are and what we are capable of. Our feelings, how we think, what we value in life and what we think or feel is important to us as an individual. Take the time to just think about that for a minute. It is important as I hear people all the time saying that they live their lives from a set point of view and won't change. That's an interesting statement as if people think they are not changing from what they are picking up every second of every day then what are they doing with all the information? We must be changing in some small way every second yet we don't feel these changes. Probably as they are so subtle that we don't feel ourselves changing or learning, but the fact of the point is, we are taking on this information and we are changing, ever so slightly but we are changing. We have to, it's the law of how we work as a human and how our brains work. Interesting? That every second of every day we are changing slightly, so in affect we are a different person to who we were probably last week, last month or last year. If we are changing and absorbing information every second, can you imagine the new neuron pathways being grown in our brains to absorb these new learnings which we are being bombarded with? If we do nothing with this notion, these new learnings will have very little significance apart from you having some random ideas that float around your consciousness before being filed away for another time. Can you imagine what would happen if you were aware of these new learnings and every evening you took five or ten minutes to reflect on what you may have learnt that day, no matter how large or small it was? You may begin to realise that every second of every day, you were acquiring something new or discovering something about yourself you didn't understand or know before. If you can, transfer these new leanings to everyday circumstances that's when you start to grow. From a spiritual point of view these leanings are coming to you at a time you need them or may need them, so, do not dismiss anything that comes to you now. New learning outcomes are more likely to happen when we take the time to explore authentic ways to transfer new learnings to present circumstances. Don't forget that we are creating new pathways in our brains all the time and if we are programmed to keep learning, older pathways no longer needed will die away leaving room for new ones to be created. I laughed when I once heard a gentleman at an adult education centre say he had to give up the class as his head was full. If this gentleman lived for 500 years, I doubt his head would even become close to being full. As we grow, our physical brains do wither and become more fragile. That's the physical, but our subconscious just keeps on absorbing and learning. Perhaps as we get older, we need to switch over to our spiritual selves to keep growing and to keep active and young, who knows what will happen then. In order to keep evolving we need to keep learning, we need to keep seeking out new thoughts and theories about us and what we are capable of, we can only do this by understanding us and this comes from taking time out to understand who you are. Take five or 10 minutes a day to look back at your day and see what new learnings you found. As always, it doesn't have to be ground shattering but just enough to know that today, you have learnt or discovered something new about you, or your environment. Keep a journal and make a note of it. Writing things down is a good way for your mind to reiterate something you are telling yourself. Of course there may be some negatives to what you have learned that day, that's okay, as if you recall a negative is just a way to show that there must be a positive to that situation or leaning, even if it's just a case of understanding what that negative is, just take the learning from it. A good saying I saw once explains this, it stated, **'I am not what happened to me, I become who I choose to become.'** I like that very much as it is stating that what happened is a learning curve which I will take on board, BUT it is my choice as to whether you let that learning change you or not. People who have read my first book will remember something I put in there that stated, *'If you think you can or if you think you cannot, then you are right in both instances.'* In other words, it is your choice as to whether you think you can do something or not. Take whichever decision you choose, but then take responsibility for your actions, you cannot blame anyone for anything you have done. Before we move on from this part, I still think it's important to understand more about the, I. We covered this earlier in book in the chapter 'What am I capable of', but let's just add the following. In discovering the 'Who Am I?', 'Being Human' and 'What Am I Capable of?' It can be made simpler if people will only engage with an understanding of themselves. In doing so, you will open a door which will reveal to you the unfolding process of this life. If you can understand the learnings you take on a day-to-day basis, it will reveal to you that we, almost all the time, react out of old habits that we think are us, rather than witnessing what we actually are, which in turn will allow us to craft our lives in the manner they should be lived. Within this realisation burns a fire, a quest to learn more and at the same time, it gives you time to look back and see that perhaps up to now you were just a flame. That is okay, as remember, a positive is born from a negative. You may feel energised and realise also that you are living from a place of fear, as let's face it, fear controls the masses, it can be taught very subtly but before we know it, it grows within our psyche and becomes us. Where do we get this fear from? Mainly the media, politicians and from kind minded people trying to point out a flaw within us, or it may be a flyaway comment or a serious conversation. Remember the saying, *'If you don't read newspapers you are not informed, if you read newspapers then you are misinformed.'* We do read them and we take on board their worries and their fears and that overtime become engrained within us. You see people are not disturbed by things, but by the view they take of them and the media does a great job at times, in changing our views of certain issues and problems as they arise to make us unsure as to what is really going on. Let's take a break from this as someone asked me today what actually is spirituality? Although we have covered this earlier in the book, it's always good to go over important points. And I think that going over spirituality is a 'must' in this last spark to make you realise that it is important for you to understand.

The term spirituality is kind of a philosophical concept that may confuse a lot of us I believe majority of people have an idea of what it means, but it still doesn't resonate with most of us, who still think it is that connection to church or to a religion. The dictionary states that it is *'The quality of being concerned with the human spirit or soul as opposed to material or physical things.'* And that for me, is spot on with what I thought it was and certainly what I was brought up to believe. As you can see, it doesn't belong to one group or another, rather than to the collective good of us all. Ah! I hear you say, yes there is still some religious teaching in that spirituality is to do with the soul. What soul are we talking about? The soul of god or our individual soul? I think this is all to do with our individual soul, or to put it another way our subconscious mind. I agree with the description from the dictionary above, but for me the soul and the spirit are one and the same, they both fall under the subconscious. Why? Because our soul is that deeper part of us, that part that lives outside of our normal day thinking. The part we covered earlier when we looked at the chapter on our senses. Remember the five senses we use every day what we touch, taste, smell, hear and see, which our conscious mind uses? Then there is the higher self, the unseen that these five basic senses are controlled by, which is the subconscious mind that resides within the unseen and is far more powerful than conscious mind. I believe science is there also, that the soul and spirit is the subconscious mind, they are one and the same. We as humans, (and because we have that tendency to need to belong to something to feel worthy), may say that the soul and spirit lives with God. I am not being blasphemous here, but the soul and spirit (subconscious) certainly lives in a higher plane but it is still you, it is the essence of who you are, as an individual. The Dalai Lama states spirituality are qualities that make us who we are and cover compassion, love, forgiveness, patience and harmony. He states that these qualities of spirituality can be cultivated within us all unlike religion, which is more of a choice, being spiritual means being who you actually are. That was from a holy leader, but science is also understanding this point. Spirituality is also being covered by science. Science is understanding that our true selves, our subconscious, is not found in being separate to those around us but rather to our connection to nature which we covered in the second chapter on 'Understanding Nature'. This awareness of our higher self being connected to the universe and to all matter that surrounds us, means that to science being spiritual is just a natural state we are constantly in. If we connect to all things with the love, compassion and harmony that the Dalai Lama states, which being spiritual invokes, then we are living at one with everything around us. I don't know about you but for me that is an incredibly powerful way to live our lives. If we all lived from this point of view, our lives would be filled with meaning. For me this makes the religious part come alive, but with an understanding that God, the universe or however you see this all being energy, is present within us now. We don't need to pray for this to come into our lives as it is already present. Again, forgive me as it is not my intention to falsify any religious teachings. So how do we become more spiritual? Let me break this down into the physical, as in who we are in the here and now, and then into the medium side. That part that I and others use to tap into the energy of others.

In order to become more spiritual, we must recognise who we are at any given time. A lot of people are already doing this and thus are probably more in tune to being spiritual than they thought they were. One of the ways to embrace who you are is to recognise that we have imperfections and that from a higher plane of living these imprecations are a part of our physical being on this earth. In other words, what we are on this earth is not who we really are on a higher non-physical plane. We are pure energy thus we are spiritual beings living a human existence. We must take this onboard and understand that this earth plane we are on now, this human experience, is just that an experience that we must embrace in order to learn what we can at this time. You chose to come here at this time, so there must be a learning you need to embrace to take forward with you. If you can get your minds around this, then this is the first step to becoming more spiritual. It is almost like an awakening to the fact that you are more than your human body.

The next realisation comes from loving yourself for who you are. It is that inner knowing that you have this inner being that is connected to everything around you. People rush around for possessions that they think gives them that higher status. It's almost like saying, I have something you don't have; therefore, I have a higher status than you. In fact, it means I have a higher stress rate and I am probably very insecure and, as a result I need material wealth. I know it isn't easy in this world we live in but try and just resign to the fact that to find confidence you just need to realise that you have an internal you, that doesn't need to be better off than the person next door. Learn to live within and then you won't have this fear of being without. Look around your home and your environment, know when enough is enough, be comfortable, but don't be over-indulgent as all this brings is stress and uncertainty. If you want to become more spiritual, then learn to listen to the inner you, those gut feelings that contain all the answers. Listen to the subconscious that is far more powerful that the conscious mind which unfortunately listens and is programmed by what people think we should have and what we should be doing.

Then we have living in the now, being present in the moment. We spend so much time looking back at the past and pondering the future, we forget that life is actually happening now. I mentioned this in my first book with a lovely little saying that said, *"The past is a memory the future a thought but now is a present,"* I like that. It takes a lot of practice to live in the here and now and letting everything else go. However, if you can master it, believe me it is incredibly powerful and brings great rewards. You will find things happen effortlessly; you get a sense of empowerment of being free. Answers to problems pop up all the time without you having to put much energy into it, and that is an important part of being spiritual, the trust that there is a greater power and energy at work, working in unison with you. Being in the now brings that unseen energy to you quicker and almost effortlessly, it is that huge library of information we seek on a day-to-day basis. If you constantly worry about yesterday and tomorrow, you are not allowing this energy to enter your life. You are shutting the door on that universal knowhow. It takes practice but when you can do this during at least some parts of your day, it does feel like miracles are happening and without any energy. Don't waste energy needlessly, just let it flow to you and through you by just being in the present moment. Then open your mind and witness God, the universe, (whatever you call this master energy), work its magic.

These simple steps will allow your mind to open to the fact that being spiritual is a natural state that we should all live from. It doesn't mean living to a set of rules, but it does mean living from that inner self and allowing you to love yourself and accepting your imperfections for what they are. Stop worrying about yesterday and tomorrow and start living for this moment. Plan your day, week year whatever it is, then let the higher subconscious work with you to bring that thing you desire. One important aspect of being spiritual is connecting to nature. Nature is spirit; it always has been and always will be and as you are connected to it, let it into your life. Go for a walk watch the birds or other wildlife, see the weather changing and feel the wind on your body. That is one way of feeling the power of nature in and around you. One point here, your DNA is different from the other seven billion people you share this life with, so what you do, think and trust will be slightly different to others. Do not allow the influence of others come into your being, this is your life no-one else's. What you find interesting will be different to everyone else. Follow your path and find that spiritual self. You don't have to believe in God or be a hippy or do anything out of the ordinary, just believe and be you. Before I finish this part on spirituality, someone asked me today, if we are spiritual? Does that mean when we die, we go to heaven? So, let me add this bit in that due to Judeo-Christianity we are scared to die, scared about death, but the ancients of Native American Indians, Incas, Mayans celebrated the end of life as a re-born into the universal spirit, where we came from before being delivered here on earth at this time. Again I ask, why and what did these ancient people know about death, yet we, as 'civilised' people, feel we have lost our way by treating death as the end, as something to be terrified of? If there were two constants for people on this earth, it is that we are all born and we will all die, the bit in-between is for you to experience as a personal journey. Passing on, which is for me a better way of saying we die, is a new chapter a new beginning. Yes, I feel for those left behind and mourning for their loved ones, as I have done, but at the same time, these loved ones have left us for a higher plane of living, they have taken their leanings and are using them for the collective good. For those of us fortunate enough to tap into this energy, we know and understand this, as did the ancients. Perhaps it is now in our time on this earth to return to the basics of who and what the ancients understood so we can go on celebrating death, as without celebrating death (which is something that we know will happen), how we can we really celebrate life? If we can learn to understand that spirituality is the connection with nature and not within a human invention of a saviour, we would again feel connected to the realm of the subconscious where our true spirit, or soul, resides. There isn't an out there, but there is a within, a place where our true self resides. This for me is the meaning of spirituality and of the true essence of who we are. Death is just an extension of us, it is a creation of a new beginning where we continue to evolve and grow. Don't follow the idea that it is the end, as science is understanding this death time is just a move into our real home and back to our true selves. I know some of you will get it and some won't. That is totally fine as this is as always, a journey for you to open and question life and your place within it. One thing I will add, as no doubt some of you will be sceptical which is normal, is that quantum mechanics is now understanding that this energy we are made from, which binds us all together is infinite, it doesn't seem to have a beginning or end. If that is the case and when our spirit or energy leaves our physical bodies, this energy must live on. It isn't a physical thing anymore as it merges with all the energy around us. That, as I have mentioned before, is what I feel I connect to when I speak, communicate or sense with those that have passed. If that is the case, then we can all communicate with our lost loved ones, it's just understanding this idea and being open to this notion. Death isn't something to be feared, it is just a part of the great journey we are on. It hurts those that are left behind, but for that person, albeit scary at the time must be enlightening. When I was at school, I went on a canoeing trip to the south of France. We were having a great time and just enjoying the incredible scenery as we canoed down the Ardeche River. We stopped for lunch one day and some friends and I decided to go swimming as it was hot and we were a little sweaty from the morning's exertions. I, being a complete idiot, thought it would be good idea to swim out to a rock that stood out on the far side of the river. The river wasn't that wide so off I went. I didn't realise how strong the current was but managed to reach the rock. On the way back, however, I found myself struggling, I went to try and rest but I felt myself being pulled away by the current. I began to panic and thrash around and began to drown. But you know what? As I felt myself being pulled down into the river, I felt a deep calming. When I managed to get to the surface for air, I felt heavy and almost like I didn't belong, when I was dragged back down again, this feeling of calm and serenity returned. I was eventually plucked from the river by one of the instructors that saw me struggling and came out in his canoe to rescue me. As he pulled me from the river and into the canoe coughing and spluttering, I remember feeling that I had been cheated I again felt heavy, confused and almost angry that I had been brought back to this air breathing existence. I have asked others that have also had these experiences and they all reported in having similar feelings of being cheated and angry by being brought back. Now it could be that at these times the body gives of some kind of hormone that makes you feel like that when you have cheated death. As when I think back to this time, the feeling of letting go and releasing myself to dying, gave me this huge sense of calm, serenity and a kind of understanding that I have never felt before or after. Before I carry on, this is a personal journey for all of us, as I disapprove of violence of any kind, this near-death experience is one that must be experienced when the time is right and not when others think it's right. I mean the act of killing another human being for whatever reason, is barbaric and Neanderthal way of being which still tells me as a race of people we are not learning and have to live from a terror point of view that killing someone is the end result. Which also means we are very insecure and really haven't learnt much from history about how to love and live together. Anyway, sorry, of my soapbox. Perhaps when I was drowning my spirit was getting to free itself of the bonds with this earth and transcend into this natural state. When I was brought back, my spirit was yet again part of heavy state of the physical, hence the heavy feeling I and others got.

It is interesting when we look back at the ancients the Mayans, Egypt and indigenous people of North and South America as they celebrated death, they didn't fear it. Some religious beliefs have huge parties when someone dies to celebrate their life and journey into the next. I will finish about death now as it is a subjective topic, but I hope I have given you some thoughts on the subject to make you think of it in a slightly different way.

At the beginning of the book, I said we were a part of nature and that we had to re-connect to nature for us as an individual and for the greater good of all. And that there are many theories and ideas about why there is so much confusion around the world at the moment? All steps from our history have led us to this point, all the ideas, theories, wars and evolution has all led to this moment in time. If everything so far has led us to this point in time, this very moment when you are reading this, then what is stopping us from achieving anything we want? Over the last few thousand years, we have grown and evolved into a global society that understands the greater good for all. It understands that if we help each other we can achieve so much. It will not recognise hunger nor poverty anymore, nothing will stop us from doing what we want, or achieving what we want to achieve. Every day will be different, an adventure to behold, to learn from, to grab with both hands and to experience that excitement of finding something new to do. Most illnesses will be eradicated as medicine strives for cures and treatments, both natural and man-made treatments. After all we develop medicine to heal and to safeguard our future children. People will laugh at the thought of having stress, instead they will talk about the excitement of that new project or idea. Natural crops will grow in the fields, as we work with nature and the sustenance she provides. Violence is a thing of the past, as we are all working together for everyone, there is no longer a need for one-upmanship or insecurities as we help each other along the way. We are striving in science, and as new discoveries are found they are shared and developed, making us all look in wonder at nature and the natural world around us and what we are learning from this amazing planet and the things on it. Furthermore, we are looking beyond us as a physical being and beginning to understand that this life we are living now is just an extension to our spiritual selves. We are all free, awake and learning to be individuals. Isn't that just an amazing place to be? So where the hell has it all gone wrong? What has happened to us to make us even more fearful than we have ever been, poverty and hunger are everyday occurrences which live alongside obesity. Cancer and heart illness are still the number one killers, oh not forgetting the new illnesses of motor neurone disease, dementia and HIV that seem to be living quite happily within our societies. Murders and violence still dominate some societies as those that are insecure like to take. We are not free as we are dominated by our work and social schedules, we have IT now that tells us when to eat when to sleep when to exercise. When I was growing up, we kept fit by playing outdoors running and going for long walks with our parents. Now we have to join expensive gyms and do the new fad of exercise that is supposed to be helping us keep in shape at an extortionate price. Is this what is meant by us evolving into a grown-up society where we are all living as one and collectively helping each other? In fact, it is getting worse not better. These days at school it seems that we are being discouraged from free thinking, as we engage more IT that takes away a lot of the essence of having a mind that also works from a common-sense point of view. Why is that? I mean, having a free mind that uses common sense to think things out is useful, eh? It allows us to stand back and question things. Ah! But there we have the answer, you see having a free open mind is not so easy to control. One way to control a population is to close down that ability to have an open mind, so instead we have confusion and we leave the rest to those higher than ourselves who we 'think' know what's best for us. Being taught common sense at schools is a thing of the past as we use a more conventional way of teaching that means we are not taught to ask questions or to ask why, instead we are taught to follow. If we follow, then we are not walking our own path, we become lemmings. In my first book, it teaches you to walk a different path from the rest. People who have read my book state that they are trying to walk their own path, but it's difficult. Of course, it is, as we are not taught to do this, we are taught to follow conventional ways of thinking and being. We can change but it is difficult, it means letting go of the way you have been taught to see the world and simply stop and look at it from another point of view. Actually, it is your point of view. The first few chapters in this book will help you with that, but the first step is to stop, be quiet and ask questions. If you ask questions, then it means you want answers, if you want answers then you are ready to listen, just ask the right people and use common sense for the answers that you seek. Nature has all the answers, you just need to engage with her and listen, the answers will come but maybe not the way you think they will. Do not become the person society thinks you should become, be the person you want to be, choose to ask and to be that person, that individual. There are people that will stop you from being that person, as they think that having a free mind is dangerous. But controlling never came to anything. As a race, we believe we are all seeing humans, but in fact we fail to see the world around us. We believe that killing justifies who we are or does it in fact just show that we are still primal in our approach to problems and issues. Politicians shout at each other and call each other liars, instead of talking collectively and productively around a table. If we were to learn compassion and love instead of war and terror, wouldn't this be a better way to live? We all seek happiness and yet most strive to find it out there, where in fact it is within us, within our very being, it is who we are. As previously mentioned, it takes more effort to be unhappy and sad than it does to be happy. More facial muscles are used to make us frown than to make us smile. Interesting to think that the happiest people on this planet are those that have the least. I could go on, but you get the idea, that to be happy is a natural state to be and uses no energy, whereas being unhappy and angry takes effort. Are we really happy? With all our technology, our mobile phones, tablets and computers? Or because of all this technology are we becoming disconnected?

We covered this earlier in the book, but I think this is an important point to cover. We seem to look up to those that dare to think differently, ask questions and challenge the way things are. These people used to be commonplace but now, due to the way we teach, we have become followers, waiting for that change, looking in anticipation to our politicians and leaders to bring about that positive change we need. How would we really know or recognise a leader these days? How would we know who is right and who is wrong as we sit and listen? Problem is the more we wait and sit and wait some more, we become restless and disillusioned with what we are being told, or in fact not told. We have forgotten how to make those changes ourselves as common sense and being allowed to ask questions is slowly being squashed by those, we rely on to make our decisions for us. You have to be that change, don't wait for it, be it, dare to think a little differently to those around you, small steps to change make a huge difference. Realise that without this change we are not creating a better world for us, we are destroying the very foundations that created us. If we keep following those that are also lost, we fall into that abyss of lies and deceit that wallows in our everyday existence. Let too much technology into our lives and we take away that crucial part of us that made the greats of the past who they were, I am talking about common sense. If we lose the ability to connect with nature and everything she gives us, we will eventually destroy our world, not the planet, as that has been around for millions of years and will continue to survive, I am talking about us. If we lose sight of what we are doing to the planet, then we lose sight of us. What will happen when we cut down that last supportive tree? I am not talking about the last living tree, but that last tree that tips the balance from us having clear air to having poisoned air? The rivers are becoming more and more polluted, the oceans full of our rubbish and non-degradable plastic, tons of the stuff. We run for charities and for making our world a better place by raising money, but are we running toward a solution or running away from the problem. We raise money, give it to the charities and then think that's my bit done. Wrong, if you want to make a difference don't run, in fact, stop. How can you make a difference? Start by using your mind and see beyond that what is being told to you. You know what I am talking about as this is in-bread in all of us, only those that like to keep taking will destroy their world. Most of us, if we are honest, are reaching a point where we know that enough is enough, we need to take back control of who we are, why we are here and where we are going. Start asking questions. See beyond the lies and the mistrust of those we look up to or vote in, to make a difference to us. I am being unfair here as there are a lot of politicians, teachers and leaders that are trying to make a difference but as they are the minority, we don't hear them. So stop, start thinking, engage with yourself get back to basics, don't follow others, start walking your own path and writing your own stories. Choose carefully the writings of others and get inspired, ask questions and then carve your story into the very being of this planet we are on. Make it a place to inspire others, to make others sit up and listen. Be you, don't hurt others along your journey but instead inject love and wisdom into those you meet. Don't take second best but be the best that you can be by being and believing in the one person you can really rely on, and that is you, no-one else but you. Technology has its place, but don't become insecure by relying on it to make your life better, as if you rely too heavily on it, it will only make you a follower of its design. You were born at this time to make a difference, to learn and to experience life. Start to experience life and let life into your being. There has never been a better time to open your mind to experience all that life has to offer. At the same time realise that this is a place to learn to experience and to make a difference for you and for those around you. When the time comes, take this learning with you to that place where we all go, where we will all meet again to swap and exchange stories on what you have learned while being on this wonderful planet. One thing, as you start to follow your own path, don't be fooled into thinking you have to know yourself well, your true identity comes from realising that each day is a journey and that as you discover yourself you will ebb and flow in tune with your surroundings and with nature. Nothing is constant and that goes for you and your emotions, sure you will have good days and bad days, this is just part of the journey. Simply celebrate the good days and learn from the bad days and just keep walking. Some people I speak to say that when they move into this place where they are 'finding themselves' they sometimes feel empty and afraid as they feel they become detached. Let me explain what emptiness is, as in fact it is far from being that empty place. Emptiness is actually a defining space, as within this space are things and these things have their own energy. By anything existing, according to physics, means that it actually exists, it creates a force within the world. Emptiness is there because of the things around it, without these things there is no emptiness, so in effect energy creates nothing as much as it creates everything. Emptiness, is just a positive or negative, depending on how you see it. Everything exists and is there for a reason, but the fact it is there means it is existing and as such is subject to change and distortion. The unseen, or that empty space, is a force which actually binds everything together. Within this space is unlimited thinking, so don't be afraid if when on your path to change you start to feel an emptiness, this just means you are on the right path. In nature, there has to be a balance remember the yin and yang, the dark the light, positive and negative and the full and the empty. Opposite forces create all the energy needed within the universe. Within these opposite forces is where the power comes from needed to create a new energy. If on your path to change you feel this emptiness, then that is good, it means you are on the right path, keep going and realise it is all a learning curve. Make the invisible visible again, by the act of connecting to your inner self. Meaning let go of the world according to others, connect to the world according to you. Only by connecting to nature can we really become the people we are supposed to be and this is so important, hence the reason I am bringing this up again. To make the invisible visible, you have to experience the oneness with the world. You do this with this re-connecting to you, go outside, watch the clouds, the birds, see the plants and trees just being and growing experience the sun and wind on your face, feel the earth beneath your feet, realise you are a part of this, it isn't out there, it is here within you. This isn't being hippy by the way, this is how we are going to survive as a race, as mentioned before nature always finds a way she has over the last millions of years and will continue to do so long after we have gone. She will replenish and she will clean up. If we don't take care of this planet, she will rebel, and as a species we will suffer and collapse; we need to take action now by stop following each other and being gullible and to start living with nature, injecting that good old common sense and learn to walk our own path. Ask questions, don't take the norm for what it is, change and allow yourself to flow and beat in time with the universe. Our task is to experience the oneness with nature and the world we live in, remember we are a part of nature and the natural state she is in. We are not apart from names as we are not a part of artificial intelligence. If we can truly experience the connection with the world around us, we will realise that to destroy the world we are only destroying us.

This part of the book is called '*The Last Spark*' and I already explained why I called it that, it is basically a call to you, to make you realise that as a human on this planet you need to help and respect it, we all need to do our little part in helping it survive. We have covered a lot in this second part and I have ranted a bit (sorry), however, I feel we need to wake up now and smell the toxicity that is causing a plague around our world. This smell is fear, of insecurities and of people taking, thinking that if they don't then they won't survive. The only survivors of this world if it ever came to it, will be those free thinkers, those that are able to think for themselves and see what we are becoming if we don't change our ways. Life always helps those that help themselves and if you start to look within and see who you really are then life will help you. I hope that by reading the first parts of this book and this last part, it has opened your mind to some new ideas.

Being a Human Whisperer is really nothing more than having a deeper understanding about us humans and the part we play within ourselves and the greater world around us. We are unique and we have evolved to this point in our history. Being guardians of our future-selves means we have to do our part to help write the story for future generations. Yet I feel and see that we haven't even started this next chapter, we engross ourselves with the technology of now not realising that this will have a negative effect on our spiritual growth. Being spiritual is one of the main parts of our psyche that we must return to if we are to become successful. This isn't hidden in the depth of time and buried with the ancients, it's here and now, and we have to embrace to bring back those qualities that makes us who we are. We are not superior to the animal or plant world, in fact we think we are clever and more adaptable, but it couldn't be further from the truth. Sorry, if this sounds like an attack on human existence, it isn't, but it may be a wakeup call. A friend of mine a few years ago had, had enough of his mundane life as an office clerk in a shipping company. He longed to be creative and put his love of cars (well engines really) to the forefront of what he wanted to do. His colleagues laughed and said he would never make anything of himself as he was clumsy and according to his boss, thick. But maybe he was clumsy and gave the appearance of being thick as he was bored and unmotivated. After one, let's say interesting week, he called me to say he had quit his job and was going to set up a garage working with classic cars. He had found a cheap garage that suited his purpose and already had his first customer, which was in fact his uncle. Nonetheless, it was a paying job working on his uncle's classic Triumph TR6. He did a good job and his uncle took him along to a Triumph Club meeting where he gave out his business cards. He got his second job there and then and as time went on, he built up his reputation and now has a specialised garage employing 12 staff members, all mad enthusiasts like him. All they do is classic cars, Triumphs, Lotus, Fords and people even ship their cars to him from all over the world. He has a wonderful garage in the Midlands (a part of the UK) and to say he is happy is putting it mildly. He makes very good money and his employees are more like family. My friend had the vision and the motivation by not liking his mundane job to make that change, he took small steps which led to his dream. I asked him if at any point he was scared it wouldn't work, he said that he was more scared by not allowing himself to follow his dream, his own path. This works on both scales; I am sure there are mechanics out there that would love the chance to work in an office. The point is that follow your dream, don't follow the crowd. I have a thought that if you take the chance to dream, then put this dream to work, life and nature works with you. It is when we procrastinate that life gives us that kick up the backside to 'get on with it', as long as you don't hurt anyone else along the way, be you, ask those questions, be different and believe in you and not those around you.

I hope this has given you some food for thought and given you an understanding that unless we personally take back control of our lives and start to live from within and not from without, then we are heading for a place we don't want to be. I will finish with a prophecy from the Cree Indian tribe,

"Only when the last tree has been cut down, and the last fish has been caught, and the last stream poisoned, we will realise we cannot eat money."